Scriptures For Survival

In the End Times

A Book of Declarations

Volume Two in the Series

Getting the Word in You!

Hebrews 4:12 For the word of God is living and powerful, and sharper than any two-edged sword, piercing even to the division of soul and spirit, and of joints and marrow, and is a discerner of the thoughts and intents of the heart.

Scriptures For Survival

In the End Times

A Book of Declarations

Volume Two in the Series

Getting the Word in You!

By Jackie May Johnson

Copyright 2014 Jackie Johnson

All rights reserved

No part of this book may be reproduced, stored in a retrieval system, scanned, or distributed in any printed or electronic form - mechanical, photocopy, recording, scanning or other - without the express prior written permission of the copyright holder.

Unless indicated otherwise, all Scripture references are taken from the New King James Version.

NKJV Copyright @1979, 1980, and 1982 by Thomas Nelson, Inc. Used by permission. All rights reserved

NIV Copyright @ 1973, 1978, 1984 by International Bible Society. Used by permission of Zondervan Publishing House. All rights reserved

Scripture quotations marked (TLB) are taken from The Living Bible copyright © 1971. Used by permission of Tyndale House Publishers, Inc., Carol Stream, Illinois 60188. All rights reserved.

The American Standard Version of the Holy Bible is in the Public Domain.

"Scripture quotations taken from the Amplified® Bible,
Copyright © 1954, 1958, 1962, 1964, 1965, 1987 by The Lockman Foundation Used by permission." (www.Lockman.org)

DEDICATION

This book is dedicated to all who want to know what God has to say in His Word about providing for us in the days we are living in. It is dedicated to all new believers, and to those who want to have strong faith in the end times.

I dedicate this book to my friend Keasha, and pray the blessings of God over her!

Lastly, I dedicate this book to my husband Bob, and to my precious sons and family, Matthew and Roseann, Ken and Rachel, David and Morgan, and Timothy, and to my grandchildren, Lydia, Ben, Charlotte and Lucy. You are the loves of my life! May you always love the Word of God!

3 John 1:4 I have no greater joy than to hear that my children walk in truth.

TABLE OF CONTENTS

ACKNOWLEDGMENTS……………………...viii

INTRODUCTION……………………….…….ix

CHAPTER ONE - God's Word; Prayer…..….1

CHAPTER TWO - Faith; Trusting God… …21

CHAPTER THREE - Direction; Guidance ….37

CHAPTER FOUR - Provision; Prosperity ….51

CHAPTER FIVE - Healing; Long Life…… …69

CHAPTER SIX - Fear Not; Protection………95

CHAPTER SEVEN - Salvation……………..115

CHAPTER EIGHT - Deliverance……………139

CHAPTER NINE - Favor, Mercy, Grace…...159

CHAPTER TEN - Restoration; Justice……..183

CONCLUSION……………………………..…209

ACKNOWLEDGMENTS

First, I thank God for sending Jesus, and giving us His written Word and His precious Holy Spirit. I am so grateful that we can have a close relationship with our God, through Jesus! I thank God for His love, and abundant kindness.

I want to thank my husband Bob for leading me to the Lord, and for all his encouragement to me in raising our family, and in everything I have done in service to the Lord. Thank you also for your many hours, and much help in formatting this book. You are a blessing, in my life, and I praise God for you!

INTRODUCTION

What is the will of God for my life? How can I walk in victory in these troubled times? God has a lot to say in His Word concerning the integrity of His Word, and concerning the times we are living in. With the threat of nuclear bombs, the changing weather patterns, and the unstable economy, we are left in a dilemma. How will we survive these end days? Our answer to that question though, should be this: By trusting in God, and in His Word! That's the answer we need for these troubled times.

I have, perhaps like many of you, made lists and lists of scriptures concerning different topics over the years. I have notebooks full of them! Even if you don't have notebooks, you probably have lists somewhere yourself! In this volume, I decided to 'organize' them in a way so that I could easily locate various scriptures. It is an answer to my question – "Now where was that scripture located again"? Each chapter deals with topics that are important; especially for the times we are living in. For example, we want to be operating out of love and faith, and not fear. So, I included every scripture I felt that was relevant on the subject of faith and on not being afraid. I did this for every chapter. Of course, it is by no means exhaustive. I chose scriptures both from the Old Testament and the New Testament. A brief declaration or confession is included with each scripture. I have deliberately not changed the scriptures, because I wanted the scripture and reference to be taken from the Bible as it is. However, you can personalize the scriptures easily if you desire to.

God's Word is true and forever settled in heaven. He is not a man that He should lie. We must come to a place where we believe God! If the water dries up, He can bring water from a rock. If there is no food, He can multiply the loaves. Even in the wilderness, their shoes never wore out, and there were no Walmarts there! Won't God meet our needs? If we are to be the overcomers that God is looking for, then we must stay in the Scriptures and meditate on them until we know what God will do.

Our spirit man is strengthened every time we speak God's Word. We are building ourselves up. If we are to be strong in our spirit, it will be necessary to continue in His Word.

Romans 10:17 So then faith comes by hearing, and hearing by the word of God.

Faith doesn't come by prayer or worship. Faith comes when we hear God's word. Faith comes by listening to the Word of God spoken and preached.

How do you get the Scriptures in your heart? You take the promises of God and you begin confessing them. What do you need in your life? Answered prayer? Direction? Healing? Provision? Restoration? Salvation for loved ones? Then these are the Scriptures for you to confess and meditate on. As you confess these Scriptures, God will hear and the angels will move on your behalf. Be diligent to confess the Scriptures that you need to have faith for. We don't have to be afraid, lacking, sick or confused! God has given us His word. These promises are given for us to live a victorious life in Christ! (For more information on making declarations, you may want to read Volume 1, <u>I Am Loved By God</u>. This book deals with the reality of who we are in Christ, and is especially good for new believers).

Introduction

It is my prayer that this book will become a useful tool for you, to locate scriptures easily. Additionally, I pray that that as you meditate on these truths and speak them over your life, you will become strong in your spirit. I pray that you will find yourself not dreading these troubled times, but instead you will be strong in the Lord, and in the power of His might. And, I pray that you will be an overcomer, doing great exploits for Jesus in our generation!

If not us, who?
If not now, when?

Blessings,
Jackie May

I AM ROYALTY! I WALK WITH DIGNITY!

I have an inheritance in Jesus Christ!
I am crowned with favor and blessings-
Because He paid the price!
He has given me all good things to enjoy,
I have authority- the devil's works I destroy.
He heals my broken heart, and sets me free
From all the clutches of the enemy.
No more shame, no more rejection!
Jesus is my hope and my protection.
I'm walking tall, with my head up high,
I'm dreaming my dream, reaching for the sky!
Intimacy with God: it belongs to me
I claim my inheritance freely
Nothing can stop me; it's a done deal
I rehearse these things- they have become real!
I see and hear my Lord all right,
I walk by faith and not by sight.
So when the lies come and tell me I'm through
I don't listen to them- this is what I do:
I pray the Word, meditate and declare
I renew my mind- I am an heir!
I receive all things, given to me
Healing, restoration and prosperity
I declare it's a brand new day-
Thank you, Lord; I will have what You say!

CHAPTER ONE

God's Word And Prayer

Psalm 119:89
Forever, O Lord, Your word is settled in heaven.

The following scriptures speak about the integrity of God's Word, and the assurance of answered prayer. His word is like a rock; it's settled. It's firm. It won't change. As we focus on His Word, it will settle our hearts. We can trust Him, because He is faithful to His Word. We need to meditate on His promises, and trust Him to answer our prayers. He has given us many scriptures that pertain to answered prayer. As you think about these promises, trust that God is faithful, and that He hears and answers. Believe Him, and He will surely bring it to pass.

You may find it helpful to answer these questions as you meditate on these promises.

1. Will God go back on His Word?
2. Can I trust His word?
3. How can I know that my prayers will be answered?
4. What conditions are there for answered prayer?
5. What did Jesus have to say about answered prayer?

CHAPTER ONE

God's Word And Prayer

1. God Doesn't Lie Or Change His Mind
Numbers 23:19
God is not a man, that He should lie, nor a son of man, that He should repent. Has He said, and will He not do? Or has He spoken, and will He not make it good?

2. I Hear The Word, And Do It, And I Am Successful
Joshua 1:8
This Book of the Law shall not depart from your mouth, but you shall meditate in it day and night, that you may observe to do according to all that is written in it. For then you will make your way prosperous, and then you will have good success.

Matthew 7:24-25
Therefore whoever hears these sayings of Mine, and does them, I will liken him to a wise man who built his house on the rock: 25 and the rain descended, the floods came, and the winds blew and beat on that house; and it did not fall, for it was founded on the rock.

3. When I Pray He Hears Me
Job 22:27
You will make your prayer to Him, He will hear you, and you will pay your vows.

Psalm 3:4
I cried to the Lord with my voice, and He heard me from His holy hill.

Psalm 34:4
I sought the Lord, and He heard me, and delivered me from all my fears.

4. **What I Declare Is Established For Me**
Job 22:28
You will also declare a thing, and it will be established for you; so light will shine on your ways.

Romans 4:17
God, who gives life to the dead and calls those things which do not exist as though they did.

5. **I Delight In The Word Of God And Meditate On It And I Prosper**
Psalm 1:1-3
Blessed is the man who walks not in the counsel of the ungodly, nor stands in the path of sinners, nor sits in the seat of the scornful; 2 But his delight is in the law of the Lord, and in His law he meditates day and night. 3 He shall be like a tree planted by the rivers of water, that brings forth its fruit in its season, whose leaf also shall not wither; and whatever he does shall prosper.

6. **I Ask For My Inheritance, And He Gives It To Me**
Psalm 2:8
Ask of Me, and I will give you the nations for Your inheritance, and the ends of the earth for Your possession.

7. **God's Word Is Perfect And Pure**
Psalm 18:30
As for God, His way is perfect; the word of the Lord is proven; He is a shield to all who trust in Him.

Psalm 19:7-8
The law of the Lord is perfect, converting the soul; the testimony of the Lord is sure, making wise the simple; 8 the statutes of the Lord are right, rejoicing the heart; the commandment of the Lord is pure, enlightening the eyes.

8. Doing God's Word Brings Reward
Psalm 19:11
Moreover by them Your servant is warned, and in keeping them there is great reward.

James 1:23-25
For if anyone is a hearer of the word and not a doer, he is like a man observing his natural face in a mirror; 24 for he observes himself, goes away, and immediately forgets what kind of man he was. 25 But he who looks into the perfect law of liberty and continues in it, and is not a forgetful hearer but a doer of the work, this one will be blessed in what he does.

9. God Speaks And It Is Done
Psalm 33:6,9
By the word of the Lord the heavens were made, and all the host of them by the breath of His mouth. 9 For He spoke, and it was done; He commanded, and it stood fast.

Numbers 23:19
Has He said, and will He not do? Or has He spoken, and will He not make it good?

Ezekiel 12:25
"For I am the Lord, I speak, and the word which I speak will come to pass; it will no more be postponed; for in your days, O rebellious house, I will say the word and

perform it," says the Lord GOD.

10. **The Word Of The Lord Is Everlasting**
Psalm 33:11
The counsel of the Lord stands forever, the plans of His heart to all generations.

Psalm 111:7-8
The works of His hands are verity and justice; all His precepts are sure. 8 They stand fast forever and ever, and are done in truth and uprightness.

Psalm 119:72
The law of Your mouth is better to me than thousands of coins of gold and silver.

Psalm 119:86
All Your commandments are faithful.

11. **God's Ears Are Open To My Prayers**
Psalm 34:15
The eyes of the Lord are on the righteous, and His ears are open to their cry.

Psalm 65:2
O You who hear prayer, to You all flesh will come.

Proverbs 15:29
The Lord is far from the wicked, but He hears the prayer of the righteous.

12. **When I Cry Out, He Hears Me**
Psalm 34:17
The righteous cry out, and the Lord hears, and delivers them out of all their troubles.

Psalm 40:1
I waited patiently for the Lord; and He inclined to me, and heard my cry.

Psalm 55:17
Evening and morning and at noon I will pray, and cry aloud, and He shall hear my voice.

Psalm 56:9
When I cry out to You, then my enemies will turn back; this I know, because God is for me.

Psalm 91:15
He shall call upon Me, and I will answer him; I will be with him in trouble; I will deliver him and honor him.

13. I Delight In The Lord, And He Gives Me The Desires Of My Heart

Psalm 10:17
Lord, You have heard the desire of the humble.

Psalm 20:4
May He grant you according to your heart's desire, and fulfill all your purpose.

Psalm 21:2
You have given him his heart's desire, and have not withheld the request of his lips. Selah.

Psalm 37:4
Delight yourself also in the Lord, and He shall give you the desires of your heart.

Psalm 145:19
He will fulfill the desire of those who fear Him.

14. As I Walk Uprightly, He Doesn't Withhold Anything From Me
Psalm 66:18-20
If I regard iniquity in my heart, the Lord will not hear.
19 But certainly God has heard me; He has attended to the voice of my prayer. 20 Blessed be God, who has not turned away my prayer, nor His mercy from me!

Psalm 84:11
No good thing will the Lord God withhold from me because I walk uprightly.

15. Angels Listen To His Word And Bring It To Pass
Psalm 103:20-21
Bless the Lord, you His angels, who excel in strength, who do His word, heeding the voice of His word. 21 Bless the Lord, all you His hosts, you ministers of His, who do His pleasure.

16. God's Word Keeps Me From Sinning
Psalm 119:9-11
How can a young man cleanse his way? By taking heed according to Your word. 10 With my whole heart I have sought You; Oh, let me not wander from Your commandments! 11 Your word I have hidden in my heart, that I might not sin against You.

17. God's Word Strengthens Me
Psalm 119:28
My soul melts from heaviness; strengthen me according to Your word.

18. I Can Trust In Your Word
Psalm 119:89
Forever, O Lord, Your word is settled in heaven.

Proverbs 30:5
Every word of God is pure; He is a shield to those who put their trust in Him.

19. **Your Words Are Truth And Life**
Psalm 119:93
I will never forget Your precepts, for by them You have given me life.

Psalm 119:99
I have more understanding than all my teachers, for Your testimonies are my meditation.

Psalm119:142
Your righteousness is an everlasting righteousness, and Your law is truth.

Psalm 119:151
You are near, O Lord, and all Your commandments are truth.

John 6:63
It is the Spirit who gives life; the flesh profits nothing. The words that I speak to you are spirit, and they are life.

20. **I Love Your Word And I Am Not Offended**
Psalm 119:165
Great peace have those who love Your law, and nothing causes them to stumble.

21. **Your Word Is Higher Than Your Name**
Psalm 138:2
I will worship toward Your holy temple, and praise Your name For Your lovingkindness and Your truth; for You have magnified Your word above all Your name.

22. The Lord Is Near To Me When I Call On Him
Psalm 145:18-19
The Lord is near to all who call upon Him, to all who call upon Him in truth. 19 He will fulfill the desire of those who fear Him; He also will hear their cry and save them.

Isaiah 55:6
Seek the Lord while He may be found, call upon Him while He is near.

23. God's Word Will Produce What He Desires
Isaiah 55:11
So shall My word be that goes forth from My mouth; it shall not return to Me void, but it shall accomplish what I please, and it shall prosper in the thing for which I sent it.

24. God Is Watching Over His Word, To See That It Is Fulfilled
Jeremiah 1:11-12 (NIV)
Then the Lord said to me, "You have seen well, for I am ready to perform My word." 12 The Lord said to me, "You have seen correctly, for I am watching to see that my word is fulfilled."

25. God's Word Is Powerful
Jeremiah 23:29
"Is not My word like a fire?" says the Lord, "And like a hammer that breaks the rock in pieces"?

26. When I Seek God, I Find Him
Jeremiah 29:11-13
For I know the thoughts that I think toward you, says the Lord, thoughts of peace and not of evil, to give you a future and a hope. 12 Then you will call upon Me and go and pray to Me, and I will listen to you. 13 And you will seek Me and find Me, when you search for Me with all your heart.

27. When I Call, He Answers Me, And Shows Me Great Things
Jeremiah 33:3
Call to Me, and I will answer you, and show you great and mighty things, which you do not know.

28. Before I Call He Hears And Answers
Isaiah 65:24
It shall come to pass, that before they call, I will answer; and while they are still speaking, I will hear.

29. God Doesn't Change
Malachi 3:6
For I am the Lord, I do not change.

30. When I Pray In Secret God Will Reward Me Openly
Matthew 6:6
But you, when you pray, go into your room, and when you have shut your door, pray to your Father who is in the secret place; and your Father who sees in secret will reward you openly.

31. Your Kingdom Come, Your Will Be Done
Matthew 6:9-13
In this manner, therefore, pray: Our Father in heaven, hallowed be Your name. 10 Your kingdom come. Your will be done on earth as it is in heaven. 11 Give us this day our daily bread. 12 And forgive us our debts, as we forgive our debtors. 13 And do not lead us into temptation, but deliver us from the evil one. For Yours is the kingdom and the power and the glory forever. Amen.

32. My Father Knows What I Need
Matthew 6:8

Therefore do not be like them. For your Father knows the things you have need of before you ask Him.

Matthew 6:32
For after all these things the Gentiles seek. For your heavenly Father knows that you need all these things.

33. As I Seek God, He Rewards Me And Answers Me
Matthew 6:33
But seek first the kingdom of God and His righteousness, and all these things shall be added to you.

Matthew 7:8
For everyone who asks receives, and he who seeks finds, and to him who knocks it will be opened.

34. I Ask, Seek, And Knock And It Is Opened For Me
Matthew 7:7
Ask, and it will be given to you; seek, and you will find; knock, and it will be opened to you.

Luke 11:9-10
So I say to you, ask, and it will be given to you; seek, and you will find; knock, and it will be opened to you. 10 For everyone who asks receives, and he who seeks finds, and to him who knocks it will be opened.

35. My Father Gives Me What I Ask For In Prayer
Matthew 7:9-11
Or what man is there among you who, if his son asks for bread, will give him a stone? 10 Or if he asks for a fish, will he give him a serpent? 11 If you then, being evil, know how to give good gifts to your children, how much more will your Father who is in heaven give good things to those who ask Him!

36. I Have Been Given The Keys To The Kingdom, To Bind And Loose
Matthew 16:19
And I will give you the keys of the kingdom of heaven, and whatever you bind on earth will be bound in heaven, and whatever you loose on earth will be loosed in heaven.

37. I Have Authority To Bind And Loose
Matthew 18:18
Assuredly, I say to you, whatever you bind on earth will be bound in heaven, and whatever you loose on earth will be loosed in heaven.

38. If Two Or Three Of Us Agree On Earth, It Is Done
Matthew 18:19-20
Again I say to you that if two of you agree on earth concerning anything that they ask, it will be done for them by My Father in heaven. 20 For where two or three are gathered together in My name, I am there in the midst of them.

39. I Speak To The Mountains And They Obey
Matthew 21:21
So Jesus answered and said to them, "Assuredly, I say to you, if you have faith and do not doubt, you will not only do what was done to the fig tree, but also if you say to this mountain, 'Be removed and be cast into the sea,' it will be done.

Mark 11:23
For assuredly, I say to you, whoever says to this mountain, 'Be removed and be cast into the sea,' and does not doubt in his heart, but believes that those things he says will be done, he will have whatever he says.

40. When I Pray, I Believe And Receive
Matthew 21:22
And whatever things you ask in prayer, believing, you will receive.

Mark 11:24
Therefore I say to you, whatever things you ask when you pray, believe that you receive them, and you will have them.

41. God's Words Will Not Pass Away
Matthew 24:35
Heaven and earth will pass away, but My words will by no means pass away.

Mark 13:31
Heaven and earth will pass away, but My words will by no means pass away.

1 Peter 1:23-25
…having been born again, not of corruptible seed but incorruptible, through the word of God which lives and abides forever, 24 because "All flesh is as grass, and all the glory of man as the flower of the grass. The grass withers, and its flower falls away, 25 but the word of the Lord endures forever." Now this is the word which by the gospel was preached to you.

Psalm 119:89-90
Forever, O Lord, Your word is settled in heaven. 90 Your faithfulness endures to all generations.

42. I Live By The Word Of God
Luke 4:4
But Jesus answered him, saying, "It is written, 'Man shall not live by bread alone, but by every word of God.'"

43. My Father Gives Me Good Gifts
Luke 11:11-13
If a son asks for bread from any father among you, will he give him a stone? Or if he asks for a fish, will he give him a serpent instead of a fish? 12 Or if he asks for an egg, will he offer him a scorpion? 13 If you then, being evil, know how to give good gifts to your children, how much more will your heavenly Father give the Holy Spirit to those who ask Him!

44. I Always Pray And Don't Faint
Luke 18:1
Then He spoke a parable to them, that men always ought to pray and not lose heart.

45. I Watch And Pray
Luke 21:36
Watch therefore, and pray always that you may be counted worthy to escape all these things that will come to pass, and to stand before the Son of Man.

Matthew 26:41
Watch and pray, lest you enter into temptation. The spirit indeed is willing, but the flesh is weak.

46. Whatever I Ask In Jesus Name, He Will Do
John 14:13
And whatever you ask in My name, that I will do, that the Father may be glorified in the Son.

John 14:14
If you ask anything in My name, I will do it.

John 15:16
You did not choose Me, but I chose you and appointed you that you should go and bear fruit, and that your fruit

should remain, that whatever you ask the Father in My name He may give you.

47. I Ask What I Desire And It Is Done For Me
John 15:7-8
If you abide in Me, and My words abide in you, you will ask what you desire, and it shall be done for you. 8 By this My Father is glorified, that you bear much fruit; so you will be My disciples.

48. Whatever I Ask The Father In Jesus Name He Will Give Me, And My Joy Will Be Full
John 16:23
And in that day you will ask Me nothing. Most assuredly, I say to you, whatever you ask the Father in My name He will give you.

John 16:24
Until now you have asked nothing in My name. Ask, and you will receive, that your joy may be full.

49. God's Word Builds Me Up And Saves My Soul
Acts 20:32
So now, brethren, I commend you to God and to the word of His grace, which is able to build you up and give you an inheritance among all those who are sanctified.

James 1:21
Therefore lay aside all filthiness and overflow of wickedness, and receive with meekness the implanted word, which is able to save your souls.

50. When I Don't Know What To Pray, The Holy Spirit Helps Me
Romans 8:26
Likewise the Spirit also helps in our weaknesses. For we

do not know what we should pray for as we ought, but the Spirit Himself makes intercession for us with groanings which cannot be uttered.

51. I Will Pray In The Spirit, And With My Understanding
1 Corinthians 14:14-15
For if I pray in a tongue, my spirit prays, but my understanding is unfruitful. 15 What is the conclusion then? I will pray with the spirit, and I will also pray with the understanding. I will sing with the spirit, and I will also sing with the understanding.

Ephesians 6:18
...praying always with all prayer and supplication in the Spirit, being watchful to this end with all perseverance and supplication for all the saints.

52. All Of His Promises Are Yes And Amen
2 Corinthians 1:20
For all the promises of God in Him are yes, and in Him amen, to the glory of God through us.

1 Kings 8:56
Blessed be the Lord, who has given rest to His people Israel, according to all that He promised. There has not failed one word of all His good promise, which He promised through His servant Moses.

53. I Pray For My Spiritual Eyes To Be Open
Ephesians 1:16-19
I do not cease to give thanks for you, making mention of you in my prayers: 17 that the God of our Lord Jesus Christ, the Father of glory, may give to you the spirit of wisdom and revelation in the knowledge of Him, 18 the eyes of your understanding being enlightened; that you

may know what is the hope of His calling, what are the riches of the glory of His inheritance in the saints, 19 and what is the exceeding greatness of His power toward us who believe, according to the working of His mighty power.

54. I Pray That I Will Be Rooted And Grounded In His Love For Me
Ephesians 3:16-20
…that He would grant you, according to the riches of His glory, to be strengthened with might through His Spirit in the inner man, 17 that Christ may dwell in your hearts through faith; that you, being rooted and grounded in love, 18 may be able to comprehend with all the saints what is the width and length and depth and height— 19 to know the love of Christ which passes knowledge; that you may be filled with all the fullness of God. 20 Now to Him who is able to do exceedingly abundantly above all that we ask or think, according to the power that works in us.

55. I Am Not Anxious; I Give God My Requests
Philippians 4:6
Be anxious for nothing, but in everything by prayer and supplication, with thanksgiving, let your requests be made known to God.

1 Peter 5:7
…casting all your care upon Him, for He cares for you.

56. I Pray Without Ceasing
1 Thessalonians 5:16-18
Rejoice always, 17 pray without ceasing, 18 in everything give thanks; for this is the will of God in Christ Jesus for you.

57. **God's Word Was Inspired By God For Our Good**
2 Timothy 3:16-17
All Scripture is given by inspiration of God, and is profitable for doctrine, for reproof, for correction, for instruction in righteousness, 17 that the man of God may be complete, thoroughly equipped for every good work.

2 Peter 1:20-21
...knowing this first, that no prophecy of Scripture is of any private interpretation, 21 for prophecy never came by the will of man, but holy men of God spoke as they were moved by the Holy Spirit.

58. **The Word Of God I Speak Is Powerful**
Hebrews 4:12
For the word of God is living and powerful, and sharper than any two-edged sword, piercing even to the division of soul and spirit, and of joints and marrow, and is a discerner of the thoughts and intents of the heart.

59. **I Boldly Come To His Throne Of Grace And Find Mercy And Grace**
Hebrews 4:16
Let us therefore come boldly to the throne of grace, that we may obtain mercy and find grace to help in time of need.

60. **I Ask, And Do Not Ask Amiss**
James 4:2-3
Yet you do not have because you do not ask. 3 You ask and do not receive, because you ask amiss.

61. **My Fervent Prayers Avail Much**
James 5:16-18
...The effective, fervent prayer of a righteous man avails much. 17 Elijah was a man with a nature like ours, and

he prayed earnestly that it would not rain; and it did not rain on the land for three years and six months. 18 And he prayed again, and the heaven gave rain, and the earth produced its fruit.

1 Peter 3:12
For the eyes of the Lord are on the righteous, and His ears are open to their prayers; but the face of the Lord is against those who do evil.

62. God Gives His Promises To Us
2 Peter 1:4
…by which have been given to us exceedingly great and precious promises, that through these you may be partakers of the divine nature, having escaped the corruption that is in the world through lust.

63. Whatever I Ask Of Him I Receive, Because I Please Him
1 John 3:21-22
Beloved, if our heart does not condemn us, we have confidence toward God. 22 And whatever we ask we receive from Him, because we keep His commandments and do those things that are pleasing in His sight.

64. I Am Confident That He Hears And Answers My Prayers
1 John 5:14-15
Now this is the confidence that we have in Him, that if we ask anything according to His will, He hears us.15 And if we know that He hears us, whatever we ask, we know that we have the petitions that we have asked of Him.

65. I Keep Myself Built Up By Praying In The Holy Spirit
Jude 1:20-21

But you, beloved, building yourselves up on your most holy faith, praying in the Holy Spirit, 21 keep yourselves in the love of God, looking for the mercy of our Lord Jesus Christ unto eternal life.

Acts 1:8
But you shall receive power when the Holy Spirit has come upon you; and you shall be witnesses to Me in Jerusalem, and in all Judea and Samaria, and to the end of the earth.

Acts 2:4
And they were all filled with the Holy Spirit and began to speak with other tongues, as the Spirit gave them utterance.

Acts 4:31
And when they had prayed, the place where they were assembled together was shaken; and they were all filled with the Holy Spirit, and they spoke the word of God with boldness.

CHAPTER TWO

Faith And Trusting God

Romans 10:17
So then faith comes by hearing, and hearing by the word of God.

Volumes of books have been written on the subject of faith. It is the foundation for our trust in God, because without faith, we can't please God. It is important to keep ourselves built up in faith. Jesus Himself asked if He would really find faith on the earth in the end. As for us, we want to be in faith. We will put these scriptures in our hearts, and trust our God. And even when our faith is tested we have all we need to overcome, because we have been given the gift of faith. We will believe something; why not believe what God has to say? Nothing is impossible for Him. Even though our possibilities are limited, His are not!

Ask yourself these questions concerning faith in God.

1. How does our faith grow?
2. Can I pray for faith?
3. Is anything too hard for the Lord?
4. How does my faith work?
5. Where is the word of faith?

CHAPTER TWO

Faith And Trusting God

1. **Nothing Is Too Hard For The Lord**
Genesis 18:14
Is anything too hard for the Lord? At the appointed time I will return to you, according to the time of life, and Sarah shall have a son.

2. **I Believe In The Lord God And His Prophets And I Prosper**
2 Chronicles 20:20
Hear me, O Judah and you inhabitants of Jerusalem: Believe in the Lord your God, and you shall be established; believe His prophets, and you shall prosper.

3. **My God Can Do Everything**
Job 42:2
I know that You can do everything, and that no purpose of Yours can be withheld from You.

4. **I Believe I Will See The Goodness Of The Lord**
Psalm 27:13
I would have lost heart, unless I had believed that I would see the goodness of the Lord in the land of the living.

5. **I Am Blessed As I Trust In The Lord**
Psalm 34:8
Oh, taste and see that the Lord is good; blessed is the man who trusts in Him!

6. **I Trust In The Lord**
Psalm 118:8-9
It is better to trust in the Lord than to put confidence in

man. 9 It is better to trust in the Lord than to put confidence in princes.

7. **He Is My Shield As I Trust Him**
Proverbs 30:5
Every word of God is pure; He is a shield to those who put their trust in Him.

8. **Nothing Is Too Hard For You**, **Lord God**
Jeremiah 32:17
Ah, Lord God! Behold, You have made the heavens and the earth by Your great power and outstretched arm. There is nothing too hard for You.

9. **I Am The Just And I Live By Faith**
Habakkuk 2:4
Behold the proud, his soul is not upright in him; but the just shall live by his faith.

Hebrews 10:38
Now the just shall live by faith; but if anyone draws back, My soul has no pleasure in him.

Romans 1:16-17
For I am not ashamed of the gospel of Christ, for it is the power of God to salvation for everyone who believes, for the Jew first and also for the Greek. 17 For in it the righteousness of God is revealed from faith to faith; as it is written, "The just shall live by faith."

10. **When Jesus Speaks The Word I Believe**
Matthew 8:10,13
When Jesus heard it, He marveled, and said to those who followed, "Assuredly, I say to you, I have not found such great faith, not even in Israel"! 13 Then Jesus said to the centurion, "Go your way; and as you have

believed, so let it be done for you." And his servant was healed that same hour.

Luke 7:7,9
But say the word, and my servant will be healed. 9 When Jesus heard these things, He marveled at him, and turned around and said to the crowd that followed Him, "I say to you, I have not found such great faith, not even in Israel!"

11. My Faith Makes Me Well
Matthew 9:22
But Jesus turned around, and when He saw her He said, "Be of good cheer, daughter; your faith has made you well." And the woman was made well from that hour.

Mark 5:34
And He said to her, "Daughter, your faith has made you well. Go in peace, and be healed of your affliction."

Luke 8:48
And He said to her, "Daughter, be of good cheer; your faith has made you well. Go in peace."

Luke 7:50
Then He said to the woman, "Your faith has saved you. Go in peace."

12. It Is Done Unto Me According To My Faith
Matthew 9:29
Then He touched their eyes, saying, "According to your faith let it be to you."

Luke 18:42
Then Jesus said to him, "Receive your sight; your faith has made you well."

Faith And Trusting God

13. **It Is Done To Me As I Desire**
Matthew 15:28
Then Jesus answered and said to her, "O woman, great is your faith! Let it be to you as you desire." And her daughter was healed from that very hour.

14. **I Have Faith To Speak To The Mountains In My Life**
Matthew 17:20
So Jesus said to them, "Because of your unbelief; for assuredly, I say to you, if you have faith as a mustard seed, you will say to this mountain, 'Move from here to there,' and it will move; and nothing will be impossible for you".

15. **With God All Things Are Possible**
Matthew 19:26
But Jesus looked at them and said to them, "With men this is impossible, but with God all things are possible."

Luke 1:37
For with God nothing will be impossible.

Luke 18:27
But He said, "The things which are impossible with men are possible with God."

16. **I Can Speak To Mountains, And They Obey**
Matthew 21:21
So Jesus answered and said to them, "Assuredly, I say to you, if you have faith and do not doubt, you will not only do what was done to the fig tree, but also if you say to this mountain, 'Be removed and be cast into the sea,' it will be done".

17. **When I Pray, In Faith I Receive**
Matthew 21:22
And whatever things you ask in prayer, believing, you will receive.

Mark 11:24
Therefore I say to you, whatever things you ask when you pray, believe that you receive them, and you will have them.

18. **Jesus Sees My Faith**
Mark 2:5
When Jesus saw their faith, He said to the paralytic, "Son, your sins are forgiven you."

19. **All Things Are Possible To Me As I Believe**
Mark 9:23
Jesus said to him, "If you can believe, all things are possible to him who believes."

20. **My Faith Makes Me Well**
Mark 10:52
Then Jesus said to him, "Go your way; your faith has made you well." And immediately he received his sight and followed Jesus on the road.

Luke 17:19
And He said to him, "Arise, go your way. Your faith has made you well."

21. **I Have Faith In God**
Mark 11:22
So Jesus answered and said to them, "Have faith in God".

22. I Speak To Mountains And They Move
Mark 11:23
For assuredly, I say to you, whoever says to this mountain, 'Be removed and be cast into the sea,' and does not doubt in his heart, but believes that those things he says will be done, he will have whatever he says.

23. Let It Be Done Unto Me According To Your Word
Luke 1:38
Then Mary said, "Behold the maidservant of the Lord! Let it be to me according to your word." And the angel departed from her.

24. I Only Believe
Luke 8:50
But when Jesus heard it, He answered him, saying, "Do not be afraid; only believe, and she will be made well."

25. I Have Faith To Speak To The Situations In My Life, And They Change
Luke 17:6
So the Lord said, "If you have faith as a mustard seed, you can say to this mulberry tree, 'Be pulled up by the roots and be planted in the sea,' and it would obey you".

26. Jesus Will Find Faith When He Returns
Luke 18:8
I tell you that He will avenge them speedily. Nevertheless, when the Son of Man comes, will He really find faith on the earth?

27. If I Believe, I Will See The Glory Of God
John 11:40
Jesus said to her, "Did I not say to you that if you would believe you would see the glory of God?"

28. I Will Do Greater Works
John 14:12
Most assuredly, I say to you, he who believes in Me, the works that I do he will do also; and greater works than these he will do, because I go to My Father.

29. Faith In Jesus Name Heals The Sick
Acts 3:11-12,16
Now as the lame man who was healed held on to Peter and John, all the people ran together to them in the porch which is called Solomon's, greatly amazed. 12 So when Peter saw it, he responded to the people: "Men of Israel, why do you marvel at this? Or why look so intently at us, as though by our own power or godliness we had made this man walk? 16 And His name, through faith in His name, has made this man strong, whom you see and know".

30. I Believe God That It Will Be Just As He Told Me
Acts 27:25
Therefore take heart, men, for I believe God that it will be just as it was told me.

31. I Call Things That Do Not Exist As Though They Did
Romans 4:17
(as it is written, "I have made you a father of many nations") in the presence of Him whom he believed—God, who gives life to the dead and calls those things which do not exist as though they did.

32. I Believe God's Promises And They Come To Pass
Romans 4:19-21
And not being weak in faith, he did not consider his own body, already dead (since he was about a hundred years

old), and the deadness of Sarah's womb. 20 He did not waiver at the promise of God through unbelief, but was strengthened in faith, giving glory to God, 21 and being fully convinced that what He has promised, He was also able to perform.

33. **I Am Justified By Faith**
Romans 5:1-2
Therefore, having been justified by faith, we have peace with God through our Lord Jesus Christ, 2 through whom also we have access by faith into this grace in which we stand, and rejoice in hope of the glory of God.

34. **The Word Of Faith Is In My Heart And Mouth**
Romans 10:8
But what does it say? "The word is near you, in your mouth and in your heart" (that is, the word of faith which we preach).

35. **I Believe And Will Never Be Put To Shame**
Romans 10:10-11
For with the heart one believes unto righteousness, and with the mouth confession is made unto salvation. 11 For the Scripture says, "Whoever believes on Him will not be put to shame."

36. **Faith Comes As I Hear The Word Of God**
Romans 10:17
So then faith comes by hearing, and hearing by the word of God.

37. **I Have Faith**
Romans 12:3
For I say, through the grace given to me, to everyone who is among you, not to think of himself more highly than he ought to think, but to think soberly, as God has

dealt to each one a measure of faith.

38. My Faith Is In The Power Of God
1 Corinthians 2:4-5
And my speech and my preaching were not with persuasive words of human wisdom, but in demonstration of the Spirit and of power, 5 that your faith should not be in the wisdom of men but in the power of God.

39. God Has Prepared Great Things For Me
1 Corinthians 2:9
But as it is written: "Eye has not seen, nor ear heard, nor have entered into the heart of man the things which God has prepared for those who love Him."

40. I Believe, Therefore I Speak
2 Corinthians 4:13
And since we have the same spirit of faith, according to what is written, "I believed and therefore I spoke," we also believe and therefore speak.

41. Things Seen Are Subject To Change By The Word Of God
2 Corinthians 4:18
While we do not look at the things which are seen, but at the things which are not seen. For the things which are seen are temporary, but the things which are not seen are eternal.

42. I Walk And Live By Faith Not By Sight
2 Corinthians 5:7
For we walk by faith, not by sight.

Galatians 2:20
I have been crucified with Christ; it is no longer I who live, but Christ lives in me; and the life which I now live in the

flesh I live by faith in the Son of God, who loved me and gave Himself for me.

43. I Receive The Promise Of The Spirit By Faith
Galatians 3:14
That the blessing of Abraham might come upon the Gentiles in Christ Jesus, that we might receive the promise of the Spirit through faith.

44. My Faith Works By My Love And Grows Exceedingly
Galatians 5:6
For in Christ Jesus neither circumcision nor uncircumcision avails anything, but faith working through love.

2 Thessalonians 1:3
We are bound to thank God always for you, brethren, as it is fitting, because your faith grows exceedingly, and the love of every one of you all abounds toward each other.

45. Christ Dwells In My Heart Through Faith
Ephesians 3:16-17
...that He would grant you, according to the riches of His glory, to be strengthened with might through His Spirit in the inner man, 17 that Christ may dwell in your hearts through faith.

46. We Are Coming To The Unity Of The Faith
Ephesians 4:13-14
...till we all come to the unity of the faith and of the knowledge of the Son of God, to a perfect man, to the measure of the stature of the fullness of Christ; 14 that we should no longer be children, tossed to and fro and carried about with every wind of doctrine, by the trickery

of men, in the cunning craftiness of deceitful plotting.

47. I Take The Shield Of Faith And Quench The Darts Of The Enemy
Ephesians 6:16
Above all, taking the shield of faith with which you will be able to quench all the fiery darts of the wicked one.

48. I Put On The Breastplate Of Faith
1 Thessalonians 5:8
But let us who are of the day be sober, putting on the breastplate of faith and love, and as a helmet the hope of salvation.

49. I Cling To My Faith In Christ
1 Timothy 1:19 (TLB)
Cling tightly to your faith in Christ and always keep your conscience clear, doing what you know is right. For some people have disobeyed their consciences and have deliberately done what they knew was wrong. It isn't surprising that soon they lost their faith in Christ after defying God like that.

50. I Fight The Good Fight Of Faith
1 Timothy 6:12
Fight the good fight of faith, lay hold on eternal life, to which you were also called and have confessed the good confession in the presence of many witnesses.

51. I Share My Faith
Philemon 1:6
...that the sharing of your faith may become effective by the acknowledgment of every good thing which is in you in Christ Jesus.

52. I Mix Faith With The Word And It Brings Results
Hebrews 4:2
For indeed the gospel was preached to us as well as to them; but the word which they heard did not profit them, not being mixed with faith in those who heard it.

53. I Hold Fast My Confession Of Faith And I Inherit The Promises
Hebrews 4:14
Seeing then that we have a great High Priest who has passed through the heavens, Jesus the Son of God, let us hold fast our confession.

Hebrews 6:12
We desire that you do not become sluggish, but imitate those who through faith and patience inherit the promises.

54. I Have A Better Covenant With Better Promises
Hebrews 8:6
But now He has obtained a more excellent ministry, inasmuch as He is also Mediator of a better covenant, which was established on better promises.

55. My Heart Is Full Of Faith
Hebrews 10:22
Let us draw near with a true heart in full assurance of faith, having our hearts sprinkled from an evil conscience and our bodies washed with pure water.

56. I Hold Fast My Confession Of Faith
Hebrews 10:23,35
Let us hold fast the confession of our hope without wavering, for He who promised is faithful. 35 Therefore

do not cast away your confidence, which has great reward.

57. I Have Faith For What I Hope For
Hebrews 11:1-3
Now faith is the substance of things hoped for, the evidence of things not seen. 2 For by it the elders obtained a good testimony. 3 By faith we understand that the worlds were framed by the word of God, so that the things which are seen were not made of things which are visible.

58. I Use My Faith And I Please Him
Hebrews 11:6
But without faith it is impossible to please Him, for he who comes to God must believe that He is, and that He is a rewarder of those who diligently seek Him.

59. Just Like Sarah, I Believe God Is Faithful To Perform His Promises For Me
Hebrews 11:11
By faith Sarah herself also received strength to conceive seed, and she bore a child when she was past the age, because she judged Him faithful who had promised.

60. I Pray In Faith
James 1:6-8
But let him ask in faith, with no doubting, for he who doubts is like a wave of the sea driven and tossed by the wind. 7 For let not that man suppose that he will receive anything from the Lord; 8 he is a double-minded man, unstable in all his ways.

61. My Faith Without Works Is Dead
James 2:18-20
But someone will say, "You have faith, and I have works."

Show me your faith without your works, and I will show you my faith by my works. 19 You believe that there is one God. You do well. Even the demons believe--and tremble! 20 But do you want to know, O foolish man, that faith without works is dead?

62. **My Prayers Of Faith Save The Sick**
James 5:15
And the prayer of faith will save the sick, and the Lord will raise him up. And if he has committed sins, he will be forgiven.

63. **My Faith Overcomes The World**
1 John 5:4-5
For whatever is born of God overcomes the world. And this is the victory that has overcome the world—our faith. 5 Who is he who overcomes the world, but he who believes that Jesus is the Son of God?

64. **I Build Myself Up On My Most Holy Faith**
Jude 1:20
But you, beloved, building yourselves up on your most holy faith, praying in the Holy Spirit.

65. **I Keep The Faith**
Revelation 14:12
Here is the patience of the saints; here are those who keep the commandments of God and the faith of Jesus.

CHAPTER THREE

Direction And Guidance

Psalm 119:105
Your word is a lamp to my feet and a light to my path.

Which way should I go? What path should I take? Will the Lord lead me? Absolutely! He is a good shepherd, and He leads His sheep. He has given us two special ways to lead us - His written Word, the Bible, and His Holy Spirit. As Christians, we are lead by the Spirit of God.

Romans 8:14 For as many as are led by the Spirit of God, these are sons of God.

His word says that He directs our steps; He leads us in the way we should go. He leads us during the day, when we sleep and when we wake up. He even guides us in times of famine, and brings us to fresh waters. He is ever with us, to lead and direct us, if we believe.

Build your faith in God's guidance for you as you answer and ponder these questions.

1. Who is it that leads me?
2. Where does He lead me?
3. How can I know He will lead me?
4. What does He lead me into?
5. When will He lead me?

CHAPTER THREE

Direction And Guidance

1. **You Gave Your Spirit To Instruct Me**
Nehemiah 9:19-20
Yet in Your manifold mercies You did not forsake them in the wilderness. The pillar of the cloud did not depart from them by day, to lead them on the road; nor the pillar of fire by night, to show them light, and the way they should go. 20 You also gave Your good Spirit to instruct them.

2. **I Walk In God's Counsel And I Succeed**
Psalm 1:1–3
Blessed is the man who walks not in the counsel of the ungodly, nor stands in the path of sinners, nor sits in the seat of the scornful; 2 but his delight is in the law of the Lord, and in His law he meditates day and night. 3 He shall be like a tree planted by the rivers of water, that brings forth its fruit in its season, whose leaf also shall not wither; and whatever he does shall prosper.

3. **You Lead Me And Make My Way Straight**
Psalm 5:8
Lead me, O Lord, in Your righteousness because of my enemies; make Your way straight before my face.

4. **The Lord Gives Me Counsel**
Psalm 16:7
I will bless the Lord who has given me counsel; my heart also instructs me in the night seasons.

5. You, Lord, Show Me The Path Of Life
Psalm 16:11
You will show me the path of life; in Your presence is fullness of joy; at Your right hand are pleasures forevermore.

6. You Will Bring Light To My Way
Psalm 18:28,32
For You will light my lamp; the Lord my God will enlighten my darkness. 32 It is God who arms me with strength, and makes my way perfect.

7. You Lead Me Beside Still Waters
Psalm 23:2
He makes me to lie down in green pastures; He leads me beside the still waters.

8. You Lead Me In Paths Of Righteousness
Psalm 23:3
He restores my soul; He leads me in the paths of righteousness For His name's sake.

9. You Lead Me In Your Truth
Psalm 25:4-5
Show me Your ways, O Lord; teach me Your paths. Lead me in Your truth and teach me, for You are the God of my salvation; on You I wait all the day.

10. You Guide And Teach Me As I Walk In Humility
Psalm 25:9
The humble He guides in justice, and the humble He teaches His way.

11. You Will Show Me Your Ways And Plans
Psalm 25:14
The secret of the Lord is with those who fear Him, and He

will show them His covenant.

12. You Lead Me In A Smooth Path
Psalm 27:11
Teach me Your way, O Lord, and lead me in a smooth path, because of my enemies.

13. You Lead And Guide Me
Psalm 31:3
For You are my rock and my fortress; therefore, for Your name's sake, lead me and guide me.

14. God Is Instructs, Teaches And Guides Me
Psalm 32:8
I will instruct you and teach you in the way you should go; I will guide you with My eye.

15. My Steps Are Ordered Of The Lord
Psalm 37:23
The steps of a good man are ordered by the Lord, and He delights in his way.

16. I Delight To Do Your Will (Your Way)
Psalm 40:8
I delight to do Your will, O my God, and Your law is within my heart.

17. God Is My Guide Forever
Psalm 48:14
For this is God, Our God forever and ever; He will be our guide even to Eternity (death).

18. You Lead Me In Hard Times
Psalm 61:2
From the end of the earth I will cry to You, when my heart is overwhelmed; lead me to the rock that is higher than I.

19. You, Lord, Guide Me With Your Counsel
Psalm 73:24
You will guide me with Your counsel, and afterward receive me to glory.

20. You Guide Me In The Wilderness
Psalm 78:52
But He made His own people go forth like sheep, and guided them in the wilderness like a flock.

21. You Guide Me, Lord
Psalm 78:72
So he shepherded them according to the integrity of his heart, and guided them by the skillfulness of his hands.

22. God Will Not Withhold Direction From Me
Psalm 84:11
For the Lord God is a sun and shield; The Lord will give grace and glory; no good thing will He withhold from those who walk uprightly.

23. You Guide Me To My Desired Place
Psalm 107:30
Then they are glad because they are quiet; so He guides them to their desired haven.

24. Your Word Is A Lamp To My Feet
Psalm 119:105
Your word is a lamp to my feet and a light to my path.

25. Anywhere I Go You Will Lead Me
Psalm 139:10
Even there Your hand shall lead me, and Your right hand shall hold me.

26. You Lead Me In The Way Everlasting
Psalm 139:24
And see if there is any wicked way in me, and lead me in the way everlasting.

27. You Lead Me In Uprightness
Psalm 143:10
Teach me to do Your will, for You are my God; Your Spirit is good. Lead me in the land of uprightness.

28. I Trust In The Lord And He Directs My Paths
Proverbs 3: 5-6
Trust in the Lord with all your heart, and lean not on your own understanding; 6 in all your ways acknowledge Him, and He shall direct your paths.

29. You Guide Me So I Won't Stumble
Proverbs 3:23
Then you will walk safely in your way, and your foot will not stumble.

Psalm 18:33
He makes my feet like the feet of deer, and sets me on my high places.

30. He Will Keep Me From Falling Into A Trap
Proverbs 3:26
For the Lord will be your confidence and will keep your foot from being caught.

31. You Lead Me In Right Paths
Proverbs 4:11
I have taught you in the way of wisdom; I have led you in right paths.

32. My Path Is Getting Brighter Every Day
Proverbs 4:18
But the path of the just is like the shining sun, that shines ever brighter unto the perfect day.

33. You Lead Me When I Walk And When I Sleep
Proverbs 6:22
When you roam, they will lead you; when you sleep, they will keep you; and when you awake, they will speak with you.

34. You Cause My Way To Prosper
Proverbs 16:3 (NKJV)
Commit your work to the Lord, then it will succeed.

Proverbs 16:3 (The Amplified Bible)
Roll your works upon the Lord [commit and trust them wholly to Him; He will cause your thoughts to become agreeable to His will, and] so shall your plans be established and succeed.

35. The Lord Directs My Steps
Proverbs 16:9 (NKJV)
A man's heart plans his way, but the Lord directs his steps.

Proverbs 16:9 (The Living Bible)
We should make plans—counting on God to direct us.

36. The Lord Decides My Ways
Proverbs 16:33 (NKJV)
The lot is cast into the lap, but its every decision is from the Lord.

Proverbs 16:33 (The Living Bible)
We toss the coin, but it is the Lord who controls its decision.

Proverbs 16:33 (The Amplified Bible)
The lot is cast into the lap, but the decision is wholly of the Lord [even the events that seem accidental are really ordered by Him].

37. **My Lord Is Excellent In Guiding Me**
Isaiah 28:29
This also comes from the Lord of hosts, who is wonderful in counsel and excellent in guidance.

38. **He Guides Me Daily**
Isaiah 30:21
Your ears shall hear a word behind you, saying, "This is the way, walk in it," whenever you turn to the right hand or whenever you turn to the left.

39. **He Leads His Flock**
Isaiah 40:11
He will feed His flock like a shepherd; He will gather the lambs with His arm, and carry them in His bosom, and gently lead those who are with young.

40. **He Leads And Makes Crooked Paths Straight**
Isaiah 42:16
I will bring the blind by a way they did not know; I will lead them in paths they have not known. I will make darkness light before them, and crooked places straight. These things I will do for them, and not forsake them.

41. He Makes Straight My Paths
Isaiah 45:2-3
I will go before you and make the crooked places straight; I will break in pieces the gates of bronze and cut the bars of iron. 3 I will give you the treasures of darkness and hidden riches of secret places, that you may know that I, the Lord, who call you by your name, am the God of Israel.

42. God Teaches Me And Directs Me
Isaiah 48:17 (NIV)
This is what the Lord says--your Redeemer, the Holy One of Israel: "I am the Lord your God, who teaches you what is best for you, who directs you in the way you should go".

43. He Leads Me To Springs Of Water
Isaiah 49:10
They shall neither hunger nor thirst, neither heat nor sun shall strike them; for He who has mercy on them will lead them, even by the springs of water He will guide them.

44. God Directs Me Every Morning
Isaiah 50:4
The Lord God has given me the tongue of the learned, that I should know how to speak a word in season to him who is weary. He awakens me morning by morning; he awakens my ear to hear as the learned.

45. The Lord Will Guide Me Continually Even In Drought
Isaiah 58:11
The Lord will guide you continually, and satisfy your soul in drought, and strengthen your bones; you shall be like a

watered garden, and like a spring of water, whose waters do not fail.

46. **You, Lord, Direct My Steps**
Jeremiah 10:23
O Lord, I know the way of man is not in himself; it is not in man who walks to direct his own steps.

47. **You Have Good Plans For Me**
Jeremiah 29:11-14
For I know the thoughts that I think toward you, says the Lord, thoughts of peace and not of evil, to give you a future and a hope.

48. **He Leads Me In A Straight Way**
Jeremiah 31:9
They shall come with weeping, and with supplications I will lead them. I will cause them to walk by the rivers of waters, in a straight way in which they shall not stumble.

49. **Let Your Will Be Done In My Life**
Matthew 6:10
Your kingdom come, your will be done, on earth as it is in heaven.

50. **You Lead Me Away From Temptation**
Matthew 6:13
And do not lead us into temptation, but deliver us from the evil one. For Yours is the kingdom and the power and the glory forever. Amen.

51. **You Guide My Feet In Peace**
Luke 1:79
To give light to those who sit in darkness and the shadow of death, to guide our feet into the way of peace.

52. You Lead Me Away From Temptation
Luke 11:4

And forgive us our sins, for we also forgive everyone who is indebted to us. And do not lead us into temptation, but deliver us from the evil one.

53. Nothing Is Hidden From Me
Luke 12:2

For there is nothing covered that will not be revealed, nor hidden that will not be known.

54. My Shepherd Leads Me
John 10:3

To him the doorkeeper opens, and the sheep hear his voice; and he calls his own sheep by name and leads them out. Romans 8:14 For as many as are led by the Spirit of God, these are sons of God.

55. I Hear The Voice Of My Shepherd And I Won't Follow A Stranger's Voice.
John 10:4-5

And when he brings out his own sheep, he goes before them; and the sheep follow him, for they know his voice. 5 Yet they will by no means follow a stranger, but will flee from him, for they do not know the voice of strangers.

56. I Hear His Voice And Follow Him
John 10:27

My sheep hear My voice, and I know them, and they follow Me.

57. The Spirit Of Truth Will Guide Me Into All Truth
John 16:13

However, when He, the Spirit of truth, has come, He will guide you into all truth; for He will not speak on His own authority, but whatever He hears He will speak.

John 14:26
But the Helper, the Holy Spirit, whom the Father will send in My name, He will teach you all things, and bring to your remembrance all things that I said to you.

58. **The Spirit Of Truth Will Show Me Things To Come**
John 16:13-14
However, when He, the Spirit of truth, has come, He will guide you into all truth; for He will not speak on His own authority, but whatever He hears He will speak; and He will tell you things to come. 14 He will glorify Me, for He will take of what is Mine and declare it to you.

59. **His Goodness Leads Me To Repent**
Romans 2:4
Or do you despise the riches of His goodness, forbearance, and longsuffering, not knowing that the goodness of God leads you to repentance?

60. **God Reveals The Hidden Things To Me**
1 Corinthians 2:9-10
But as it is written: "Eye has not seen, nor ear heard, nor have entered into the heart of man the things which God has prepared for those who love Him." 10 But God has revealed them to us through His Spirit. For the Spirit searches all things, yes, the deep things of God.

61. **I Have The Mind Of Christ**
1 Corinthians 2:16
For "who has known the mind of the Lord that he may instruct Him?" But we have the mind of Christ.

62. God Always Leads Me In Triumph In Christ
2 Corinthians 2:14
Now thanks be to God who always leads us in triumph in Christ, and through us diffuses the fragrance of His knowledge in every place.

63. He Opens My Eyes And Guides Me
Ephesians 1:17-19
That the God of our Lord Jesus Christ, the Father of glory, may give to you the spirit of wisdom and revelation in the knowledge of Him, 18 the eyes of your understanding being enlightened; that you may know what is the hope of His calling, what are the riches of the glory of His inheritance in the saints.

64. I Will Hear His Voice; I Keep My Heart Soft And Open To Hear Him
Hebrews 3:7-8
Therefore, as the Holy Spirit says: "Today, if you will hear His voice, 8 do not harden your hearts as in the rebellion".

65. He Will Lead Me To Living Waters
Revelation 7:17
For the Lamb who is in the midst of the throne will shepherd them and lead them to living fountains of waters. And God will wipe away every tear from their eyes.

CHAPTER FOUR

Provision And Prosperity

Romans 8:32
He who did not spare His own Son, but delivered Him up for us all, how shall He not with Him also freely give us all things?

Our God is a giving God. He freely gave us Jesus; His precious Son. What would He not give us? He made a promise in the beginning- if we obey Him, He will bless us. This promise still stands. He desires good things for His children. He meets all of our needs. He is a kind, giving God.

Scripture also declares that Abraham was the Father of our faith. God blessed him and made him rich. This promise of Abraham is also to the heirs.
Galatians 3:29 And if you are Christ's, then you are Abraham's seed, and heirs according to the promise.

Answer these questions on God's will for your prosperity as you read the chapter.

1. How do we know that God will to bless us?
2. What qualifies us to receive blessings?
3. Does God care if we have our needs met?
4. Will God meet my needs?
5. Is God the God of 'more than enough'?

CHAPTER FOUR

Provision And Prosperity

1. God Is Blessing Me
Genesis 12:2-3
I will make you a great nation; I will bless you and make your name great; and you shall be a blessing. 3 I will bless those who bless you, and I will curse him who curses you; and in you all the families of the earth shall be blessed.

2. God Is The Almighty God; The El Shaddai, The All Sufficient One
Genesis 17:1-2
When Abram was ninety-nine years old, the Lord appeared to Abram and said to him, "I am Almighty God; walk before Me and be blameless. 2 And I will make My covenant between Me and you, and will multiply you exceedingly."

3. My God Is Jehovah Jireh; The Lord Who Provides
Genesis 22:8,14
And Abraham said, "My son, God will provide for Himself the lamb for a burnt offering." So the two of them went together. 14 And Abraham called the name of the place, The-Lord-Will-Provide; as it is said to this day, "In the Mount of the Lord it shall be provided".

4. As I Sow, I Also Reap
Genesis 26:12-14
Then Isaac sowed in that land, and reaped in the same year a hundredfold; and the Lord blessed him. 13 The man began to prosper, and continued prospering until he became very prosperous; 14 for he had possessions of

flocks and possessions of herds and a great number of servants.

5. **God Is Making Me 1,000 Times More**
Deuteronomy 1:11
May the Lord God of your fathers make you a thousand times more numerous than you are, and bless you as He has promised you!

6. **God Is Multiplying Me As I Obey Him**
Deuteronomy 6:1-3,10-11
Now this is the commandment, and these are the statutes and judgments which the Lord your God has commanded to teach you, that you may observe them in the land which you are crossing over to possess, 2 that you may fear the Lord your God, to keep all His statutes and His commandments which I command you, you and your son and your grandson, all the days of your life, and that your days may be prolonged. 3 Therefore hear, O Israel, and be careful to observe it, that it may be well with you, and that you may multiply greatly as the Lord God of your fathers has promised you—'a land flowing with milk and honey.' 10 So it shall be, when the Lord your God brings you into the land of which He swore to your fathers, to Abraham, Isaac, and Jacob, to give you large and beautiful cities which you did not build, 11 houses full of all good things, which you did not fill, hewn-out wells which you did not dig, vineyards and olive trees which you did not plant—when you have eaten and are full.

7. **God Gives Me The Power To Get Wealth**
Deuteronomy 8:18
And you shall remember the Lord your God, for it is He who gives you power to get wealth, that He may establish His covenant which He swore to your fathers, as it is this day.

8. The Blessings Of God Are Overtaking Me
Deuteronomy 28:2-8,11-13
And all these blessings shall come upon you and overtake you, because you obey the voice of the Lord your God: 3 "Blessed shall you be in the city, and blessed shall you be in the country. 4 "Blessed shall be the fruit of your body, the produce of your ground and the increase of your herds, the increase of your cattle and the offspring of your flocks. 5 "Blessed shall be your basket and your kneading bowl. 6 "Blessed shall you be when you come in, and blessed shall you be when you go out. 7 "The Lord will cause your enemies who rise against you to be defeated before your face; they shall come out against you one way and flee before you seven ways. 8 "The Lord will command the blessing on you in your storehouses and in all to which you set your hand, and He will bless you in the land which the Lord your God is giving you. 11 And the Lord will grant you plenty of goods, in the fruit of your body, in the increase of your livestock, and in the produce of your ground, in the land of which the Lord swore to your fathers to give you. 12 The Lord will open to you His good treasure, the heavens, to give the rain to your land in its season, and to bless all the work of your hand. You shall lend to many nations, but you shall not borrow.13 And the Lord will make you the head and not the tail; you shall be above only, and not be beneath, if you heed the commandments of the Lord your God, which I command you today, and are careful to observe them".

9. As I Keep God's Laws He Prospers Me
Deuteronomy 29:9
Therefore keep the words of this covenant, and do them, that you may prosper in all that you do.

1 Kings 2:3
And keep the charge of the Lord your God: to walk in His ways, to keep His statutes, His commandments, His judgments, and His testimonies, as it is written in the Law of Moses, that you may prosper in all that you do and wherever you turn.

10. I Choose Life And Blessings
Deuteronomy 30:15-16,19
See, I have set before you today life and good, death and evil, 16 in that I command you today to love the Lord your God, to walk in His ways, and to keep His commandments, His statutes, and His judgments, that you may live and multiply; and the Lord your God will bless you in the land which you go to possess. 19 I call heaven and earth as witnesses today against you, that I have set before you life and death, blessing and cursing; therefore choose life, that both you and your descendants may live.

11. I Keep His Words And Meditate On Them, And I Am Prosperous
Joshua 1:8
This Book of the Law shall not depart from your mouth, but you shall meditate in it day and night, that you may observe to do according to all that is written in it. For then you will make your way prosperous, and then you will have good success.

Psalm 1:1-3
Blessed is the man who walks not in the counsel of the ungodly, nor stands in the path of sinners, nor sits in the seat of the scornful; 2 But his delight is in the law of the Lord, and in His law he meditates day and night. 3 He shall be like a tree planted by the rivers of water, that

brings forth its fruit in its season, whose leaf also shall not wither; and whatever he does shall prosper.

12. **I Believe In The Prophets And I Prosper**
2 Chronicles 20:20
So they rose early in the morning and went out into the Wilderness of Tekoa; and as they went out, Jehoshaphat stood and said, "Hear me, O Judah and you inhabitants of Jerusalem: Believe in the Lord your God, and you shall be established; believe His prophets, and you shall prosper."

Ezra 6:14 So the elders of the Jews built, and they prospered through the prophesying of Haggai the prophet and Zechariah the son of Iddo.

13. **As Long As I Seek The Lord I Will Prosper**
2 Chronicles 26:5
He sought God in the days of Zechariah, who had understanding in the visions of God; and as long as he sought the Lord, God made him prosper.

2 Chronicles 31:21
And in every work that he began in the service of the house of God, in the law and in the commandment, to seek his God, he did it with all his heart. So he prospered.

Psalm 34:10
The young lions lack and suffer hunger; but those who seek the Lord shall not lack any good thing.

14. **I Shall Not Lack Anything; For You Are My Shepherd And You Give Me An Abundance**
Psalm 23:1,5

The Lord is my shepherd; I shall not want. 5 You anoint my head with oil; my cup runs over.

15. I Fear God (Walk Uprightly) And I Have No Lack
Psalm 34:9
Oh fear the Lord, you His saints! There is no want to those who fear Him.

Psalm 84:11
No good thing will He withhold from me as I walk uprightly.

16. God Takes Pleasure In Prospering Me
Psalm 35:27
Let them shout for joy and be glad, who favor my righteous cause; and let them say continually, "Let the Lord be magnified, who has pleasure in the prosperity of His servant."

17. I Have Never Lacked For Bread
Psalm 37:25
I have been young, and now am old; yet I have not seen the righteous forsaken, nor his descendants begging bread.

18. You God Cause Me To Come To My Wealthy Place Psalm 66:12
You have caused men to ride over our heads; we went through fire and through water; but You brought us out to rich fulfillment. (a wealthy place; place of abundance)

19. The Lord Daily Blesses Me
Psalm 68:19
Blessed be the Lord, who daily loads me with benefits, the God of our salvation! Selah

20. As I Delight In God's Laws, I Am Blessed
Psalm 112:1,3,9
Blessed is the man who fears the Lord, who delights greatly in His commandments. 3 Wealth and riches will be in his house, and his righteousness endures forever. 9 He has dispersed abroad, he has given to the poor; his righteousness endures forever; his horn will be exalted with honor.

21. The Lord Is Increasing Me More And More
Psalm 115:14-16
May the Lord give you increase more and more, you and your children. 15 May you be blessed by the Lord, who made heaven and earth. 16 The heaven, even the heavens, are the Lord's; but the earth He has given to the children of men.

22. Send Prosperity, Lord
Psalm 118:25
Save now, I pray, O Lord; O Lord, I pray, send now prosperity.

23. Prosperity And Peace Are In My House
Psalm 122:7
Peace be within your walls, prosperity within your palaces.

24. As I Give The First Fruits I Am Blessed
Proverbs 3:9-10
Honor the Lord with your possessions, and with the first fruits of all your increase; 10 So your barns will be filled with plenty, and your vats will overflow with new wine.

25. Riches And Honor Are With Me
Proverbs 8:18-19, 21

Riches and honor are with me, enduring riches and righteousness. 19 My fruit is better than gold, yes, than fine gold, and my revenue than choice silver. 21 That I may cause those who love me to inherit wealth, that I may fill their treasuries.

26. **The Blessing Of God Makes Me Rich**
Proverbs 10:22
The blessing of the Lord makes one rich, and He adds no sorrow with it.

27. **As I Give It, Is Given To Me**
Proverbs 11:25
The generous soul will be made rich, and he who waters will also be watered himself.

28. **The Hand Of The Diligent Makes One Rich**
Proverbs 13:4
The soul of a lazy man desires, and has nothing; but the soul of the diligent shall be made rich.

Proverbs 13:11
Wealth gained by dishonesty will be diminished, but he who gathers by labor will increase.

Proverbs 10:4
He who has a slack hand becomes poor, but the hand of the diligent makes rich.

29. **The Sinner's Wealth Is Stored Up For Me**
Proverbs 13:22
A good man leaves an inheritance to his children's children, but the wealth of the sinner is stored up for the righteous.

Ecclesiastes 2:26
For God gives wisdom and knowledge and joy to a man who is good in His sight; but to the sinner He gives the work of gathering and collecting, that he may give to him who is good before God.

30. **In My House Is Much Treasure**
Proverbs 15:6
In the house of the righteous there is much treasure, but in the revenue of the wicked is trouble.

31. **Through Knowledge And Humility Prosperity Comes To Me**
Proverbs 22:4
By humility and the fear of the Lord are riches and honor and life.

Proverbs 24:4
By knowledge the rooms are filled with all precious and pleasant riches.

32. **As I Remember The Poor, I Always Have Enough**
Proverbs 28:27
He who gives to the poor will not lack, but he who hides his eyes will have many curses.

Proverbs 19:17
He who has pity on the poor lends to the Lord, and He will pay back what he has given.

33. **I Obey God And Prosper**
Job 36:11
If they obey and serve Him, they shall spend their days in prosperity, and their years in pleasures.

Isaiah 1:19
If you are willing and obedient, you shall eat the good of the land.

34. **God Restores And Brings Double**
Job 42:10
And the Lord restored Job's losses when he prayed for his friends. Indeed the Lord gave Job twice as much as he had before.

35. **God Is Giving Me The Treasures Of Darkness**
Isaiah 45:2-3
I will go before you and make the crooked places straight; I will break in pieces the gates of bronze and cut the bars of iron. 3 I will give you the treasures of darkness and hidden riches of secret places, that you may know that I, the Lord, who call you by your name, Am the God of Israel.

36. **God Teaches Me To Profit**
Isaiah 48:17
Thus says the Lord, your Redeemer, The Holy One of Israel: "I am the Lord your God, who teaches you to profit, who leads you by the way you should go".

37. **I Shall Possess Double**
Isaiah 61:7
Instead of your shame you shall have double honor, and instead of confusion they shall rejoice in their portion. Therefore in their land they shall possess double; everlasting joy shall be theirs.

38. **As I Trust In The Lord, I Will Prosper**
Jeremiah 17:7-8
Blessed is the man who trusts in the Lord, and whose

hope is the Lord. 8 For he shall be like a tree planted by the waters, which spreads out its roots by the river, and will not fear when heat comes; but its leaf will be green, and will not be anxious in the year of drought, nor will cease from yielding fruit.

Proverbs 28:20,25
A faithful man will abound with blessings, but he who hastens to be rich will not go unpunished. 25 He who is of a proud heart stirs up strife, but he who trusts in the Lord will be prospered.

39. I Shall Eat In Plenty And Be Satisfied
Joel 2:24,26
The threshing floors shall be full of wheat, and the vats shall overflow with new wine and oil. 26 You shall eat in plenty and be satisfied, and praise the name of the Lord your God, who has dealt wondrously with you; and My people shall never be put to shame.

40. The Silver And Gold Belong To God
Haggai 2:8-9
'The silver is Mine, and the gold is Mine,' says the Lord of hosts. 9 'The glory of this latter temple shall be greater than the former,' says the Lord of hosts.

41. God Causes Me To Be Prosperous
Zechariah 8:12
For the seed shall be prosperous, the vine shall give its fruit, the ground shall give her increase, and the heavens shall give their dew—I will cause the remnant of this people to possess all these.

42. As I Bring My Tithes, The Heavens Are Opened
Malachi 3:10-12
"Bring all the tithes into the storehouse, that there may be

food in My house, and try Me now in this," says the Lord of hosts, "If I will not open for you the windows of heaven and pour out for you such blessing that there will not be room enough to receive it. 11 "And I will rebuke the devourer for your sakes, so that he will not destroy the fruit of your ground, nor shall the vine fail to bear fruit for you in the field," says the Lord of hosts; 12 "And all nations will call you blessed, for you will be a delightful land," says the Lord of hosts.

43. **As I Seek His Kingdom, All Things Are Added**
Matthew 6:19-21,33

Do not lay up for yourselves treasures on earth, where moth and rust destroy and where thieves break in and steal; 20 but lay up for yourselves treasures in heaven, where neither moth nor rust destroys and where thieves do not break in and steal. 21 For where your treasure is, there your heart will be also. 33 But seek first the kingdom of God and His righteousness, and all these things shall be added to you.

44. **God Is Able To Multiply Food**
Matthew 14:16-19

But Jesus said to them, "They do not need to go away. You give them something to eat." 17 And they said to Him, "We have here only five loaves and two fish." 18 He said, "Bring them here to Me." 19 Then He commanded the multitudes to sit down on the grass. And He took the five loaves and the two fish, and looking up to heaven, He blessed and broke and gave the loaves to the disciples; and the disciples gave to the multitudes.

45. **Good Stewards Are Rewarded**
Matthew 25:23, 28-29

His lord said to him, 'Well done, good and faithful servant; you have been faithful over a few things, I will make you ruler over many things. Enter into the joy of your lord.' 28 Therefore take the talent from him, and give it to him who has ten talents. 29 'For to everyone who has, more will be given, and he will have abundance; but from him who does not have, even what he has will be taken away.

46. **God Promises A Return Sown Seed**
Mark 4:8, 20
But other seed fell on good ground and yielded a crop that sprang up, increased and produced: some thirtyfold, some sixty, and some a hundred." 20 But these are the ones sown on good ground, those who hear the word, accept it, and bear fruit: some thirtyfold, some sixty, and some a hundred."

47. **Whoever Has Left Family For The Gospel Will Receive A Hundred-Fold**
Mark 10:29-30
Assuredly, I say to you, there is no one who has left house or brothers or sisters or father or mother or wife or children or lands, for My sake and the gospel's, 30 who shall not receive a hundredfold now in this time--houses and brothers and sisters and mothers and children and lands, with persecutions--and in the age to come, eternal life.

Matthew 19:29
And everyone who has left houses or brothers or sisters or father or mother or wife or children or lands, for My name's sake, shall receive a hundredfold, and inherit eternal life.

48. **As I Give, It Is Given Unto Me In Abundance**
Luke 6:38
Give, and it will be given to you: good measure, pressed

down, shaken together, and running over will be put into your bosom. For with the same measure that you use, it will be measured back to you.

49. It Is The Father's Good Pleasure To Give Me The Kingdom
Luke 12:7,32
But the very hairs of your head are all numbered. Do not fear therefore; you are of more value than many sparrows. 32 "Do not fear, little flock, for it is your Father's good pleasure to give you the kingdom".

Matthew 6:26
Look at the birds of the air, for they neither sow nor reap nor gather into barns; yet your heavenly Father feeds them. Are you not of more value than they?

50. As I Am Faithful In Little, He Gives Me More
Luke 16:10
He who is faithful in what is least is faithful also in much; and he who is unjust in what is least is unjust also in much.

51. Jesus Came To Give Me An Abundant Life
John 10:10
The thief does not come except to steal, and to kill, and to destroy. I have come that they may have life, and that they may have it more abundantly.

52. I Reign In Life
Romans 5:17
For if by the one man's offense death reigned through the one, much more those who receive abundance of grace and of the gift of righteousness will reign in life through the One, Jesus Christ.

53. God Gives Me Freely All Things
Romans 8:32
He who did not spare His own Son, but delivered Him up for us all, how shall He not with Him also freely give us all things?

54. The Minister Of The Word Is Worthy Of His Hire
1 Corinthians 9:11
If we have sown spiritual things for you, is it a great thing if we reap your material things?

55. Jesus Was Made Poor So I Could Be Made Rich
2 Corinthians 8:9
For you know the grace of our Lord Jesus Christ, that though He was rich, yet for your sakes He became poor, that you through His poverty might become rich.

56. I Sow Bountifully And Reap Bountifully, And Grace Abounds To Me So That I Always Have An Abundant Supply
2 Corinthians 9:6-8
But this I say: He who sows sparingly will also reap sparingly, and he who sows bountifully will also reap bountifully. 7 So let each one give as he purposes in his heart, not grudgingly or of necessity; for God loves a cheerful giver. 8 And God is able to make all grace abound toward me, that I, always having all sufficiency in all things, may have an abundance for every good work.

Ecclesiastes 11:1 (The Living Bible)
Cast your bread upon the waters, for you will find it after many days. 1 Give generously, for your gifts will return to you later.

Galatians 6:7

Do not be deceived, God is not mocked; for whatever a man sows, that he will also reap.

57. He Supplies And Multiplies My Seed
2 Corinthians 9:9-11

As it is written: "He has dispersed abroad, He has given to the poor; His righteousness endures forever." 10 Now may He who supplies seed to the sower, and bread for food, supply and multiply the seed you have sown and increase the fruits of your righteousness, 11 while you are enriched in everything for all liberality, which causes thanksgiving through us to God.

58. Abraham's Blessings Are Mine
Galatians 3:14, 29

That the blessing of Abraham might come upon the Gentiles in Christ Jesus, that we might receive the promise of the Spirit through faith. 29 And if you are Christ's, then you are Abraham's seed, and heirs according to the promise.

59. What I Sow I Reap
Galatians 6:7

Do not be deceived, God is not mocked; for whatever a man sows, that he will also reap.

60. I Am Blessed With All Spiritual Blessings
Ephesians 1:3

Blessed be the God and Father of our Lord Jesus Christ, who has blessed us with every spiritual blessing in the heavenly places in Christ.

61. God Meets All My Needs
Philippians 4:19
And my God shall supply all my need according to His riches in glory by Christ Jesus.

62. God Wills That I Prosper
3 John 2
Beloved, I pray that you may prosper in all things and be in health, just as your soul prospers.

63. God Gives Me All Things Richly To Enjoy
1 Timothy 6:17
Command those who are rich in this present age not to be haughty, nor to trust in uncertain riches but in the living God, who gives us richly all things to enjoy.

64. He Has Given Me All Things That Pertain To Life
2 Peter 1:3
As His divine power has given to us all things that pertain to life and godliness, through the knowledge of Him who called us by glory and virtue.

65. I Lack Nothing; Every Good Gift Comes From God
James 1:4,17
But let patience have its perfect work, that you may be perfect and complete, lacking nothing. 17 Every good gift and every perfect gift is from above, and comes down from the Father of lights, with whom there is no variation or shadow of turning.

CHAPTER FIVE

Healing And Long Life

1 Peter 2:24
Who Himself bore my sins in His own body on the tree, that I, having died to sins, might live for righteousness-- by whose stripes I was healed.

God says in His Word that His desire is to give us a long life. And, He has always made provision for healing for us.

Under the New Covenant, we have a better covenant with better promises. We now carry the power of God, in us, in earthen vessels. Now, we do the works of Jesus! Jesus spoke the word, and healing came. Sometimes He laid hands on folks. Other times, they were healed by their faith. Aren't we glad that there is more than one way to be healed?

As you meditate on the healing scriptures, you can substitute your name for Jesus name! You are Jesus' body on the earth now.

1. What does the Old Covenant say about our healing?
2. How can I know God's will for healing?
3. What does the New Covenant say about healing?
4. What did Jesus think about healing?
5. What is my job as a believer in Christ?

CHAPTER FIVE

Healing And Long Life

1. **The Lord Is My Healer**
Exodus 15:26
If you diligently heed the voice of the Lord your God and do what is right in His sight, give ear to His commandments and keep all His statutes, I will put none of the diseases on you which I have brought on the Egyptians. For I am the Lord who heals you.

2. **Long Life Is Mine Because I Obey My Parents In The Lord**
Exodus 20:12
Honor your father and your mother, that your days may be long upon the land which the Lord your God is giving you.

Ephesians 6:1-3
Children, obey your parents in the Lord, for this is right. 2 "Honor your father and mother," which is the first commandment with promise: 3 "that it may be well with you and you may live long on the earth."

3. **As I Serve The Lord, Sickness Is Taken From My Midst**
Exodus 23:25
So you shall serve the Lord your God, and He will bless your bread and your water. And I will take sickness away from the midst of you.

4. **God Always Makes Provision For Healing**
Numbers 21:9

So Moses made a bronze serpent, and put it on a pole; and so it was, if a serpent had bitten anyone, when he looked at the bronze serpent, he lived.

5. **As I Walk In God's Commands, My Life Will Be Long And Prosperous**
Deuteronomy 5:33
You shall walk in all the ways which the Lord your God has commanded you, that you may live and that it may be well with you, and that you may prolong your days in the land which you shall possess.

6. **The Lord Will Take Sickness Away From Me**
Deuteronomy 7:14,15
You shall be blessed above all peoples; there shall not be a male or female barren among you or among your livestock. 15 And the Lord will take away from you all sickness, and will afflict you with none of the terrible diseases of Egypt which you have known, but will lay them on all those who hate you.

7. **I Choose Life And Blessing**
Deuteronomy 30:19
I call heaven and earth as witnesses today against you, that I have set before you life and death, blessing and cursing; therefore choose life, that both you and your descendants may live.

8. **I Love My God, Obey His Voice, And He Gives Me Long Life**
Deuteronomy 30:20
That you may love the Lord your God, that you may obey His voice, and that you may cling to Him, for He is your life and the length of your days.

9. I Will Live A Long Life, With Riches And Honor
1 Chronicles 29:28
So he died in a good old age, full of days and riches and honor; and Solomon his son reigned in his place.

Job 5:26
You shall come to the grave at a full age, as a sheaf of grain ripens in its season.

10. I Called To My God And He Healed Me
Psalm 30:2
O Lord my God, I cried out to You, and You healed me.

Jeremiah 17:14
Heal me, Oh Lord and I will be healed; save me and I will be saved, for You are my praise!

11. God Delivers Me Out Of All Destruction; Not One Of My Bones Is Broken
Psalms 34:19-20
Many are the afflictions of the righteous, but the Lord delivers him out of them all. 20 He guards all his bones; not one of them is broken.

12. The Lord Sustains And Strengthens Me In My Sickness
Psalms 41:3
The Lord will strengthen him on his bed of illness; You will sustain him on his sickbed.

Isaiah 40:31
But those who wait on the Lord shall renew their strength; they shall mount up with wings like eagles, they shall run and not be weary, they shall walk and not faint.

13. **I Will Live A Long Life, By God And His Word**
Psalm 90:10
The days of my life are seventy years, and if by reason of strength eighty.

Proverbs 9:11
For by me your days will be multiplied, and years of life will be added to you.

Proverbs 10:27
The fear of the LORD prolongs days, but the years of the wicked will be shortened.

Proverbs 3:2
For length of days and long life and peace they will add to you.

Proverbs 3:16
Length of days *is* in her right hand, in her left hand riches and honor.

14. **Because God Is My Refuge, No Plague Will Come Upon Me, And I Will Live Long**
Psalm 91:9-10,16
Because you have made the Lord, who is my refuge, even the Most High, your dwelling place, 10 no evil shall befall you, nor shall any plague come near your dwelling. 16 With long life I will satisfy him, and show him My salvation."

15. **I Don't Forget God's Benefits; He Heals All My Diseases**
Psalm 103:2,3
Bless the Lord, O my soul, and forget not all His benefits: 3 who forgives all your iniquities, who heals all your diseases.

16. God's Will Is That I Am Not Weak
Psalm 105:37
He also brought them out with silver and gold, and there was none feeble among His tribes.

Hebrews 12:12-13
Therefore strengthen the hands which hang down, and the feeble knees, 13 and make straight paths for your feet, so that what is lame may not be dislocated, but rather be healed.

17. God Sent His Word And Healed Me
Psalm 107:20
He sent His word and healed them, and delivered them from their destructions.

18. I Shall Live And Not Die
Psalms 118:17
I shall not die, but live, and declare the works of the Lord.

19. The Lord Heals The Blind
Psalm 146:8
The Lord opens the eyes of the blind; The Lord raises those who are bowed down; The Lord loves the righteous.

20. He Heals Broken Hearts And Binds Up Wounds
Psalm 147:3
He heals the brokenhearted and binds up their wounds.

21. I Fear The Lord And It Brings Me Health And Strength
Proverbs 3:7-8
Do not be wise in your own eyes; fear the Lord and depart from evil. 8 It will be health to your flesh, and strength to your bones.

22. I Keep God's Words Before My Eyes And They Are Life And Health To Me

Proverbs 4:20-22

My son, give attention to my words; incline your ear to my sayings. 21 Do not let them depart from your eyes; keep them in the midst of your heart; 22 for they are life to those who find them, and health to all their flesh.

23. My Tongue Brings Health To My Body

Proverbs 12:18

There is one who speaks like the piercings of a sword, but the tongue of the wise promotes health.

Proverbs 15:4

A wholesome tongue is a tree of life, but perverseness in it breaks the spirit.

Proverbs 16:24

Pleasant words are like a honeycomb, sweetness to the soul and health to the bones.

Proverbs 18:21

Death and life are in the power of the tongue, and those who love it will eat its fruit.

24. My Heart Is Sound And Merry And It Brings Me Health

Proverbs 14:30

A sound heart is life to the body, but envy is rottenness to the bones.

Proverbs 17:22

A merry heart does good like medicine, but a broken spirit dries the bones.

25. **My God Strengthens My Bones**
Proverbs 15:30
The light of the eyes rejoices the heart, and a good report makes the bones healthy.

Isaiah 58:11
The Lord will guide you continually, and satisfy your soul in drought, and strengthen your bones; you shall be like a watered garden, and like a spring of water, whose waters do not fail.

Psalm 6:2
Have mercy on me, O Lord, for I am weak; O Lord, heal me, for my bones are troubled.

26. **By His Stripes I Am Healed**
Isaiah 53:4-5
Surely He has borne our griefs and carried our sorrows; yet we esteemed Him stricken, smitten by God, and afflicted. 5 But He was wounded for our transgressions, He was bruised for our iniquities; the chastisement for our peace was upon Him, and by His stripes we are healed.

1 Peter 2:24
Who Himself bore my sins in His own body on the tree, that I, having died to sins, might live for righteousness-- by whose stripes I was healed.

27. **My Healing Comes Quickly After Fasting**
Isaiah 58:8
Then your light shall break forth like the morning, your healing shall spring forth speedily.

28. **God Restores My Health, And Brings Healing Of My Wounds**
Jeremiah 30:17

'For I will restore health to you and heal you of your wounds,' says the Lord.

Jeremiah 33:6
Behold, I will bring it health and healing; I will heal them and reveal to them the abundance of peace and truth.

29. **I Fear God And He Brings Healing To Me**
Malachi 4:2
But to you who fear My name The Sun of Righteousness shall arise with healing in His wings; and you shall go out and grow fat like stall-fed calves.

30. **Jesus Heals Skin Conditions**
Matthew 8:2-3
And behold, a leper came and worshiped Him, saying, "Lord, if You are willing, You can make me clean." 3 Then Jesus put out His hand and touched him, saying, "I am willing; be cleansed." Immediately his leprosy was cleansed.

Mark 1:40-42
Now a leper came to Him, imploring Him, kneeling down to Him and saying to Him, "If You are willing, You can make me clean." 41 Then Jesus, moved with compassion, stretched out His hand and touched him, and said to him, "I am willing; be cleansed." 42 As soon as He had spoken, immediately the leprosy left him, and he was cleansed

Luke 5:12-13
And it happened when He was in a certain city, that behold, a man who was full of leprosy saw Jesus; and he fell on his face and implored Him, saying, "Lord, if You are willing, You can make me clean." 13 Then He put out His hand and touched him, saying, "I am willing; be

cleansed." Immediately the leprosy left him.

2 Kings 5:9-11,14
Then Naaman went with his horses and chariot, and he stood at the door of Elisha's house. 10 And Elisha sent a messenger to him, saying, "Go and wash in the Jordan seven times, and your flesh shall be restored to you, and you shall be clean." 11 But Naaman became furious, and went away and said, "Indeed, I said to myself, 'He will surely come out to me, and stand and call on the name of the Lord his God, and wave his hand over the place, and heal the leprosy.' 14 So he went down and dipped seven times in the Jordan, according to the saying of the man of God; and his flesh was restored like the flesh of a little child, and he was clean.

31. Jesus Only Speaks The Word And Healing Comes
Matthew 8:8,13
The centurion answered and said, "Lord, I am not worthy that You should come under my roof. But only speak a word, and my servant will be healed. 13 Then Jesus said to the centurion, "Go your way; and as you have believed, so let it be done for you." And his servant was healed that same hour.

Luke 7:2, 7, 9-10
And a certain centurion's servant, who was dear to him, was sick and ready to die. 7 But say the word, and my servant will be healed. 9 When Jesus heard these things, He marveled at him, and turned around and said to the crowd that followed Him, "I say to you, I have not found such great faith, not even in Israel!" 10 And those who were sent, returning to the house, found the servant well who had been sick.

32. Jesus Already Took My Sickness
Matthew 8:17
That it might be fulfilled which was spoken by Isaiah the prophet, saying: "He Himself took our infirmities and bore our sicknesses".

33. I Touch Jesus, And Through Faith I Am Made Whole
Matthew 9:20-22
And suddenly, a woman who had a flow of blood for twelve years came from behind and touched the hem of His garment. 21 For she said to herself, "If only I may touch His garment, I shall be made well." 22 But Jesus turned around, and when He saw her He said, "Be of good cheer, daughter; your faith has made you well." And the woman was made well from that hour.

Mark 5:27,28,33,34
When she heard about Jesus, she came behind Him in the crowd and touched His garment. 28 For she said, "If only I may touch His clothes, I shall be made well." 33 But the woman, fearing and trembling, knowing what had happened to her, came and fell down before Him and told Him the whole truth. 34 And He said to her, "Daughter, your faith has made you well. Go in peace, and be healed of your affliction."

Luke 8:48
And He said to her, "Daughter, be of good cheer; your faith has made you well. Go in peace."

34. I Believe You Can Heal Me, Jesus
Matthew 9:27-29
When Jesus departed from there, two blind men followed Him, crying out and saying, "Son of David, have mercy on

us!" 28 And when He had come into the house, the blind men came to Him. And Jesus said to them, "Do you believe that I am able to do this?" They said to Him, "Yes, Lord." 29 Then He touched their eyes, saying, "According to your faith let it be to you."

35. **Jesus Heals Me Of Every Sickness And Disease**
Matthew 4:23-24
And Jesus went about all Galilee, teaching in their synagogues, preaching the gospel of the kingdom, and healing all kinds of sickness and all kinds of disease among the people. 24 Then His fame went throughout all Syria; and they brought to Him all sick people who were afflicted with various diseases and torments, and those who were demon-possessed, epileptics, and paralytics; and He healed them.

Matthew 9:35
Then Jesus went about all the cities and villages, teaching in their synagogues, preaching the gospel of the kingdom, and healing every sickness and every disease among the people.

36. **I Go And Demonstrate The Kingdom**
Matthew 10:1
And when He had called His twelve disciples to Him, He gave them power over unclean spirits, to cast them out, and to heal all kinds of sickness and all kinds of disease.

Matthew 10:7-8
And as you go, preach, saying, 'The kingdom of heaven is at hand.' 8 Heal the sick, cleanse the lepers, raise the dead, cast out demons. Freely you have received, freely give.

37. **The Kingdom Is Demonstrated Through Me**
Matthew 11:5
The blind see and the lame walk; the lepers are cleansed and the deaf hear; the dead are raised up and the poor have the gospel preached to them. 6 And blessed is he who is not offended because of Me."

38. **Jesus Heals Because Of His Great Compassion**
Matthew 14:14
And when Jesus went out He saw a great multitude; and He was moved with compassion for them, and healed their sick.

39. **Through My God The Dead Are Raised**
2 Kings 13:21
So it was, as they were burying a man, that suddenly they spied a band of raiders; and they put the man in the tomb of Elisha; and when the man was let down and touched the bones of Elisha, he revived and stood on his feet.

Mark 5:36,39,41,42
As soon as Jesus heard the word that was spoken, He said to the ruler of the synagogue, "Do not be afraid; only believe." 39 When He came in, He said to them, "Why make this commotion and weep? The child is not dead, but sleeping." 41 Then He took the child by the hand, and said to her, "Talitha, cumi," which is translated, "Little girl, I say to you, arise." 42 Immediately the girl arose and walked, for she was twelve years of age.

Luke 8:49-50, 52-55
While He was still speaking, someone came from the ruler of the synagogue's house, saying to him, "Your daughter is dead. Do not trouble the Teacher." 50 But

when Jesus heard it, He answered him, saying, "Do not be afraid; only believe, and she will be made well. 52 Now all wept and mourned for her; but He said, "Do not weep; she is not dead, but sleeping." 53 And they ridiculed Him, knowing that she was dead. 54 But He put them all outside, took her by the hand and called, saying, "Little girl, arise." 55 Then her spirit returned, and she arose immediately. And He commanded that she be given something to eat.

40. I Am A Disciple Of Jesus; I Cast Out Devils And Heal The Sick
Mark 6:13
And they cast out many devils, and anointed with oil many that were sick, and healed them.

41. Whoever Jesus Touched Was Made Well
Matthew 8:16
When evening had come, they brought to Him many who were demon-possessed. And He cast out the spirits with a word, and healed all who were sick.

Mark 6:56
Wherever He entered, into villages, cities, or the country, they laid the sick in the marketplaces, and begged Him that they might just touch the hem of His garment. And as many as touched Him were made well.

42. Jesus Heals The Deaf And Mute
Mark 7:34-37
Then looking up to heaven, He sighed, and said to him, "Ephphatha," that is, "Be opened." 35 Immediately his ears were opened, and the impediment of his tongue was loosed, and he spoke plainly. 36 Then He commanded them that they should tell no one; but the more He

Healing And Long Life

commanded them, the more widely they proclaimed it. 37 And they were astonished beyond measure, saying, "He has done all things well. He makes both the deaf to hear and the mute to speak."

43. **Jesus Heals The Blind**
Matthew 20:29-34

Now as they went out of Jericho, a great multitude followed Him. 30 And behold, two blind men sitting by the road, when they heard that Jesus was passing by, cried out, saying, "Have mercy on us, O Lord, Son of David!" 31 Then the multitude warned them that they should be quiet; but they cried out all the more, saying, "Have mercy on us, O Lord, Son of David!" 32 So Jesus stood still and called them, and said, "What do you want Me to do for you?" 33 They said to Him, "Lord, that our eyes may be opened." 34 So Jesus had compassion and touched their eyes. And immediately their eyes received sight, and they followed Him.

Matthew 21:14

Then the blind and the lame came to Him in the temple, and He healed them.

Mark 8:22-26

Then He came to Bethsaida; and they brought a blind man to Him, and begged Him to touch him. 23 So He took the blind man by the hand and led him out of the town. And when He had spit on his eyes and put His hands on him, He asked him if he saw anything. 24 And he looked up and said, "I see men like trees, walking." 25 Then He put His hands on his eyes again and made him look up. And he was restored and saw everyone clearly. 26 Then He sent him away to his house, saying, "Neither go into the town, nor tell anyone in the town."

John 9:6-7
When He had said these things, He spat on the ground and made clay with the saliva; and He anointed the eyes of the blind man with the clay. 7 And He said to him, "Go, wash in the pool of Siloam" (which is translated, Sent). So he went and washed, and came back seeing.

44. **My Faith Makes Me Whole**
Mark 10:51-52
So Jesus answered and said to him, "What do you want Me to do for you?" The blind man said to Him, "Rabboni, that I may receive my sight." 52 Then Jesus said to him, "Go your way; your faith has made you well." And immediately he received his sight and followed Jesus on the road.

Luke 18: 40-43
So Jesus stood still and commanded him to be brought to Him. And when he had come near, He asked him, 41 saying, "What do you want Me to do for you?" He said, "Lord, that I may receive my sight." 42 Then Jesus said to him, "Receive your sight; your faith has made you well." 43 And immediately he received his sight, and followed Him, glorifying God. And all the people, when they saw it, gave praise to God.

45. **Believers Will Heal The Sick In Jesus Name**
Mark 16:17-18
And these signs will follow those who believe: In My name they will cast out demons; they will speak with new tongues; 18 they will take up serpents; and if they drink anything deadly, it will by no means hurt them; they will lay hands on the sick, and they will recover.

Luke 9:1-2, 6
Then He called His twelve disciples together and gave them power and authority over all demons, and to cure diseases. 2 He sent them to preach the kingdom of God and to heal the sick. 6 So they departed and went through the towns, preaching the gospel and healing everywhere.

Luke 10:9
And heal the sick that are there, and say to them, the kingdom of God is come near to you.

46. He Has Sent Me To Heal The Broken Hearted And The Blind
Luke 4:18-19
The Spirit of the Lord is upon me, because He has anointed me to preach the gospel to the poor; He has sent me to heal the brokenhearted, to proclaim liberty to the captives, and recovery of sight to the blind, to set at liberty those who are oppressed, 19 to proclaim the acceptable year of the Lord.

47. Jesus Rebukes Fevers
Matthew 8:14-15
Now when Jesus had come into Peter's house, He saw his wife's mother lying sick with a fever. 15 So He touched her hand, and the fever left her. And she arose and served them.

Luke 4:38-39
Now He arose from the synagogue and entered Simon's house. But Simon's wife's mother was sick with a high fever, and they made request of Him concerning her. 39 So He stood over her and rebuked the fever, and it left her. And immediately she arose and served them.

48. Jesus Healed Them All

Matthew 12:15
But when Jesus knew it, He withdrew from there. And great multitudes followed Him, and He healed them all.

Matthew 14:14
And when Jesus went out He saw a great multitude; and He was moved with compassion for them, and healed their sick.

Matthew 14:35-36
And when the men of that place recognized Him, they sent out into all that surrounding region, brought to Him all who were sick, 36 and begged Him that they might only touch the hem of His garment. And as many as touched it were made perfectly well.

Matthew 15:30
Then great multitudes came to Him, having with them the lame, blind, mute, maimed, and many others; and they laid them down at Jesus' feet, and He healed them.

Luke 4:40
When the sun was setting, all those who had any that were sick with various diseases brought them to Him; and He laid His hands on every one of them and healed them.

Luke 5:15
However, the report went around concerning Him all the more; and great multitudes came together to hear, and to be healed by Him of their infirmities.

Luke 6:19
And the whole multitude sought to touch Him, for there went power out of Him and He healed them all.

49. Jesus Heals The Lame
Luke 5:23-25
Which is easier, to say, 'Your sins are forgiven you,' or to say, 'Rise up and walk'? 24 But that you may know that the Son of Man has power on earth to forgive sins"—He said to the man who was paralyzed, "I say to you, arise, take up your bed, and go to your house." 25 Immediately he rose up before them, took up what he had been lying on, and departed to his own house, glorifying God.

John 5:8-9
Jesus said to him, "Rise, take up your bed and walk." 9 And immediately the man was made well, took up his bed, and walked.

Acts 3:6-8 And Peter said, silver and gold I do not have, but what I do have I give you; in the name of Jesus Christ of Nazareth, rise up and walk. 7 And he took him by the right hand and lifted him up, and immediately his feet and ankle bones received strength. 8 So he, leaping up, stood and walked and entered the temple with them—walking, leaping, and praising God.

50. Jesus Heals Hands
Luke 6:10
And when He had looked around at them all, He said to the man, "Stretch out your hand." And he did so, and his hand was restored as whole as the other.

1 Kings 13:6-7
Then the king answered and said to the man of God, "Please entreat the favor of the Lord your God, and pray for me, that my hand may be restored to me." So the man of God entreated the Lord, and the king's hand was restored to him, and became as before.

51. **Jesus Raises The Dead**
Luke 7:13-15
When the Lord saw her, He had compassion on her and said to her, "Do not weep." 14 Then He came and touched the open coffin, and those who carried him stood still. And He said, "Young man, I say to you, arise." 15 So he who was dead sat up and began to speak. And He presented him to his mother.

John 11:14,15,17,21-23, 38-44
Then Jesus said to them plainly, "Lazarus is dead. 15 And I am glad for your sakes that I was not there, that you may believe. Nevertheless let us go to him." 17 So when Jesus came, He found that he had already been in the tomb four days. 21 Now Martha said to Jesus, "Lord, if You had been here, my brother would not have died. 22 But even now I know that whatever You ask of God, God will give You." 23 Jesus said to her, "Your brother will rise again." 38 Then Jesus, again groaning in Himself, came to the tomb. It was a cave, and a stone lay against it. 39 Jesus said "Take away the stone." 40 Jesus said to her, "Did I not say to you that if you would believe you would see the glory of God?" 41 Then they took away the stone from the place where the dead man was lying. And Jesus lifted up His eyes and said, "Father, I thank You that You have heard Me. 42 And I know that You always hear Me, but because of the people who are standing by I said this, that they may believe that You sent Me." 43 Now when He had said these things, He cried with a loud voice, "Lazarus, come forth!" 44 And he who had died came out bound hand and foot with graveclothes, and his face was wrapped with a cloth. Jesus said to them, "Loose him, and let him go."

52. Jesus Brought The Kingdom To Earth
Luke 7:22

Jesus answered and said to them, "Go and tell John the things you have seen and heard: that the blind see, the lame walk, the lepers are cleansed, the deaf hear, the dead are raised, the poor have the gospel preached to them".

53. Jesus Delivers Me From Every Sickness
Luke 13:11-13,16

And behold, there was a woman who had a spirit of infirmity eighteen years, and was bent over and could in no way raise herself up. 12 But when Jesus saw her, He called her to Him and said to her, "Woman, you are loosed from your infirmity." 13 And He laid His hands on her, and immediately she was made straight, and glorified God. 16 So ought not this woman, being a daughter of Abraham, whom Satan has bound—think of it—for eighteen years, be loosed from this bond on the Sabbath?"

54. As The Early Disciples Performed Signs And Wonders, So Do I
Acts 5:12

And through the hands of the apostles many signs and wonders were done among the people.

Acts 6:8

And Stephen, full of faith and power, did great wonders and signs among the people.

Acts 8:7

For unclean spirits, crying with a loud voice, came out of many who were possessed; and many who were paralyzed and lame were healed.

Acts 9:33-34
There he found a certain man named Aeneas, who had been bedridden eight years and was paralyzed. 34 And Peter said to him, "Aeneas, Jesus the Christ heals you. Arise and make your bed." Then he arose immediately.

Acts 14:9-10
This man heard Paul speaking. Paul, observing him intently and seeing that he had faith to be healed, 10 said with a loud voice, "Stand up straight on your feet!" And he leaped and walked.

Acts 19:11-12
Now God worked unusual miracles by the hands of Paul, 12 so that even handkerchiefs or aprons were brought from his body to the sick, and the diseases left them and the evil spirits went out of them.

55. Jesus Went About Healing All
Acts 10:38
God anointed Jesus with the Holy Spirit and with power, who went about doing good and healing all who were oppressed by the devil, for God was with Him.

56. God Heals Me By My Faith, Just Like He Healed Abraham And Sarah By Their Faith
Romans 4:19-21
And not being weak in faith, he did not consider his own body, already dead (since he was about a hundred years old), and the deadness of Sarah's womb. 20 He did not waver at the promise of God through unbelief, but was strengthened in faith, giving glory to God, 21 and being fully convinced that what He had promised He was also able to perform.

Hebrews 11:11
By faith Sarah herself also received strength to conceive seed, and she bore a child when she was past the age, because she judged Him faithful who had promised.

57. **I Am Free From The Law Of Death**
Romans 8:2
For the law of the Spirit of life in Christ Jesus has made me free from the law of sin and death.

58. **The Holy Spirit Gives Life To My Body**
Romans 8:11
But if the Spirit of Him who raised Jesus from the dead dwells in you, He who raised Christ from the dead will also give life to your mortal bodies through His Spirit who dwells in you.

59. **I Discern Correctly The Lord's Body And Live**
1 Corinthians 11:29-31
For he who eats and drinks in an unworthy manner eats and drinks judgment to himself, not discerning the Lord's body. 30 For this reason many are weak and sick among you, and many sleep. 31 For if we would judge ourselves, we would not be judged.

60. **As We Pray For One Another, Healing Comes**
James 5:14-15
Is anyone among you sick? Let him call for the elders of the church, and let them pray over him, anointing him with oil in the name of the Lord. 15 Confess your faults one to another and pray for one another, that you may be healed. The effectual fervent prayer of a righteous man avails much.

61. Jesus Came To Destroy The Works Of The Devil
1 John 3:8
For this purpose the Son of God was manifested, that He might destroy the works of the devil.

John 10:10
The thief does not come except to steal, and to kill, and to destroy. I have come that they may have life, and that they may have it more abundantly.

62. Christ Has Redeemed Me From The Curse Of The Sickness
Galatians 3:13,14, 29
Christ has redeemed us from the curse of the law, having become a curse for us (for it is written, "Cursed is everyone who hangs on a tree"), 14 that the blessing of Abraham might come upon the Gentiles in Christ Jesus, that we might receive the promise of the Spirit through faith. 29 And if you are Christ's, then you are Abraham's seed, and heirs according to the promise.

63. My Soul Prospers And I Am In Health
3 John 2
Beloved, I pray that you may prosper in all things and be in health, just as your soul prospers.

1 Thessalonians 5:23
Now may the God of peace Himself sanctify you completely; and may your whole spirit, soul, and body be preserved blameless at the coming of our Lord Jesus Christ.

64. Jesus Heals Today Just Like He Did When He Lived On The Earth
Hebrews 13:8
Christ is the same yesterday, today, and forever.

65. He Provides Healing For The Nations
Revelation 22:2
In the middle of its street, and on either side of the river, was the tree of life, which bore twelve fruits, each tree yielding its fruit every month. The leaves of the tree were for the healing of the nations.

CHAPTER SIX

Fear Not And Protection

John 17:15
I do not pray that You should take them out of the world, but that You should keep them from the evil one.

When I was looking in the scriptures about not being afraid, I found over 200 scriptures. It has been said that there is a scripture for every day of the year on not being afraid. What do we need to fear? God is on our side. The enemy is already defeated. From Genesis to Revelation, we see God's hand of protection on His children. He has several ways to protect us. His angels are camped around us. We are protected by the blood of Jesus. His Holy Spirit warns us of things to come. He gives us dreams in the night, to warn us. Like a watchful Father, our God is every ready to guard His sons and daughters, and to keep them from any harm.

As you examine the protection scriptures, you may want to answer the following questions.

1. How can I be sure God will protect me?
2. Why should I not fear in troubled times?
3. Should I be afraid of men?
4. How can I appropriate God's protection?
5. What was the mission of Jesus?

CHAPTER SIX

Fear Not And Protection

1. I Am Not Afraid; God Is My Shield
Genesis 15:1
After these things the word of the Lord came to Abram in a vision, saying, "Do not be afraid, Abram. I am your shield, your exceedingly great reward."

2. I Am Not Afraid; For As He Was With Abraham, So Is God With Me
Genesis 26:24
And the Lord appeared to him the same night and said, "I am the God of your father Abraham; do not fear, for I am with you. I will bless you and multiply your descendants for My servant Abraham's sake."

3. I Am Not Afraid
Exodus 14:13
And Moses said to the people, "Do not be afraid. Stand still, and see the salvation of the Lord, which He will accomplish for you today. For the Egyptians whom you see today, you shall see again no more forever".

4. I Am Not Afraid Or Discouraged
Deuteronomy 1:21,29,30
'Look, the Lord your God has set the land before you; go up and possess it, as the Lord God of your fathers has spoken to you; do not fear or be discouraged.' 29-30 "Then I said to you, 'Do not be terrified, or afraid of them. 30 The Lord your God, who goes before you, He will fight for you, according to all He did for you in Egypt before your eyes'.

5. I Will Not Fear My Enemies; For My God Will Fight For Me
Deuteronomy 3:22
You must not fear them, for the Lord your God Himself fights for you.

6. I Am Strong And Of Good Courage; I Will Not Fear
Deuteronomy 31:6
Be strong and of good courage, do not fear nor be afraid of them; for the Lord your God, He is the One who goes with you. He will not leave you nor forsake you.

7. He Will Not Leave Me Or Forsake Me
Joshua 1:5
No man shall be able to stand before you all the days of your life; as I was with Moses, so I will be with you. I will not leave you nor forsake you.

Hebrews 13:5
Let your conduct be without covetousness; be content with such things as you have. For He Himself has said, "I will never leave you nor forsake you."

8. I Am Strong And Of Good Courage; I Am Not Afraid, For My God Is With Me
Joshua 1:9
Have I not commanded you? Be strong and of good courage; do not be afraid, nor be dismayed, for the Lord your God is with you wherever you go.

Joshua 10:25
Then Joshua said to them, "Do not be afraid, nor be dismayed; be strong and of good courage, for thus the Lord will do to all your enemies against whom you fight."

9. I Am Not Afraid, For Those With Us Are More Than Those Against Us
2 Kings 6:16
So he answered, "Do not fear, for those who are with us are more than those who are with them."

2 Chronicles 32:7
"Be strong and courageous; do not be afraid nor dismayed before the king of Assyria, nor before all the multitude that *is* with him; for *there are* more with us than with him.

10. God Is Keeping Me From Evil
1 Chronicles 4:10
And Jabez called on the God of Israel saying, "Oh, that You would bless me indeed, and enlarge my territory, that Your hand would be with me, and that You would keep me from evil, that I may not cause pain!" So God granted him what he requested.

11. I Will Not Fear For My God Is Fighting My Battles For Me.
2 Chronicles 20:15
And he said, "Listen, all you of Judah and you inhabitants of Jerusalem, and you, King Jehoshaphat! Thus says the Lord to you: 'Do not be afraid nor dismayed because of this great multitude, for the battle is not yours, but God's'.

12. I Have A Hedge Of Protection Around Me
Job 1:9-10
So Satan answered the Lord and said, "Does Job fear God for nothing? 10 Have You not made a hedge around him, around his household, and around all that he has on every side? You have blessed the work of his hands, and his possessions have increased in the land".

13. **I Will Not Be Afraid Of 10,000 People Against Me**
Psalm 3:6
I will not be afraid of ten thousands of people who have set themselves against me all around.

Psalm 91:7-8
A thousand may fall at your side, and ten thousand at your right hand; but it shall not come near you. 8 Only with your eyes shall you look and see the reward of the wicked.

Leviticus 26:8
Five of you shall chase a hundred, and a hundred of you shall put ten thousand to flight; your enemies shall fall by the sword before you.

Deuteronomy 32:30
How could one chase a thousand, and two put ten thousand to flight, unless their Rock had sold them, and the Lord had surrendered them?

14. **God Keeps Me Safe**
Psalm 4:8
I will both lie down in peace, and sleep; for You alone, O Lord, make me dwell in safety.

Proverbs 12:28
In the way of righteousness is life, and in its pathway there is no death.

15. **My God Protects Me Under The Shadow Of His Wings**
Psalm 17:8
Keep me as the apple of Your eye; hide me under the shadow of Your wings.

Psalm 36:7
How precious is Your lovingkindness, O God! Therefore the children of men put their trust under the shadow of Your wings.

Psalm 91:1,4
He who dwells in the secret place of the Most High shall abide under the shadow of the Almighty. 4 He shall cover you with His feathers, and under His wings you shall take refuge; His truth shall be your shield and buckler.

Psalm 57:1
And in the shadow of Your wings I will make my refuge, until these calamities have passed by.

Psalm 61:4
I will abide in Your tabernacle forever; I will trust in the shelter of Your wings. Selah

Psalm 63:7
Because You have been my help, therefore in the shadow of Your wings I will rejoice.

16. I Do Not Fear; My God Is My Rock Of Salvation
Psalm 18:2
The Lord is my rock and my fortress and my deliverer; my God, my strength, in whom I will trust; my shield and the horn of my salvation, my stronghold.

Psalm 18:46
The Lord lives! Blessed be my Rock! Let the God of my salvation be exalted.

Psalm 89:26
He shall cry to Me, 'You are my Father, My God, and the rock of my salvation.'

2 Samuel 22:47
The Lord lives! Blessed be my Rock! Let God be exalted, The Rock of my salvation!

Isaiah 44:8
Do not fear, nor be afraid, have I not told you from that time, and declared it? You are My witnesses. Is there a God besides Me? Indeed there is no other Rock; I know not one.

17. **He Keeps My Foot From Slipping**
Psalm 18:36
You enlarged my path under me, so my feet did not slip.

Psalm 94:18
If I say, "My foot slips," Your mercy, O Lord, will hold me up.

Psalm 91:12
In their (Angels) hands they shall bear you up, lest you dash your foot against a stone.

2 Samuel 22:37
You enlarged my path under me; so my feet did not slip.

Psalm 66:8-9
Oh, bless our God, you peoples! And make the voice of His praise to be heard, 9 who keeps our soul among the living, and does not allow our feet to be moved.

Psalm 56:13
For You have delivered my soul from death. Have You not kept my feet from falling, that I may walk before God in the light of the living?

Psalm 121:3
He will not allow your foot to be moved; He who keeps you will not slumber.

Luke 4:10-11
For it is written: 'He shall give His angels charge over you, to keep you,' 11 "and, 'In their hands they shall bear you up, lest you dash your foot against a stone.' "

18. I Will Fear No Evil, For God Is With Me
Psalm 23:4-5
Yea, though I walk through the valley of the shadow of death, I will fear no evil; for You are with me; Your rod and Your staff, they comfort me. 5 You prepare a table before me in the presence of my enemies; You anoint my head with oil; my cup runs over.

19. In Time Of War I Am Not Afraid
Psalm 27:1,3
The Lord is my light and my salvation; whom shall I fear? The Lord is the strength of my life; of whom shall I be afraid? 3 Though an army may encamp against me, my heart shall not fear; though war should rise against me, in this I will be confident.

20. He Is My Rock, My Fortress And My Refuge In Times Of Trouble
Psalm 27:5
For in the time of trouble He shall hide me in His pavilion; in the secret place of His tabernacle He shall hide me; He shall set me high upon a rock.

Psalm 31:2
Be my rock of refuge, a fortress of defense to save me. 3 For You are my rock and my fortress.

2 Samuel 22:2-3; Psalm 18:2
And he said:" The Lord is my rock and my fortress and my deliverer; 3 The God of my strength, in whom I will trust; my shield and the horn of my salvation, my stronghold and my refuge; my Savior, You save me from violence.

Psalm 62:6-7
He only is my rock and my salvation; He is my defense; I shall not be moved. 7 In God is my salvation and my glory; the rock of my strength, and my refuge, is in God.

Psalm 71:3
Be my strong refuge, to which I may resort continually; You have given the commandment to save me, for You are my rock and my fortress.

Psalm 91:2
I will say of the Lord, "He is my refuge and my fortress; my God, in Him I will trust."

Psalm 144:2
My lovingkindness and my fortress, my high tower and my deliverer, my shield and the One in whom I take refuge, who subdues my people under me.

21. **The Angel Of The Lord Guards Me**
Psalm 34:7
The angel of the Lord encamps all around those who fear Him, and delivers them.

Psalm 91:11
For He shall give His angels charge over you, to keep you in all your ways.

22. I Will Not Fear In Troubled Times
Psalm 46:1-3
God is our refuge and strength, a very present help in trouble. 2 Therefore we will not fear, even though the earth be removed, and though the mountains be carried into the midst of the sea; 3 though its waters roar and be troubled, though the mountains shake with its swelling.

23. I Will Not Be Afraid In Evil Days
Psalm 49:5
Why should I fear in the days of evil, when the iniquity at my heels surrounds me?

24. I Am Not Afraid Of Man; I Trust In God
Psalm 56:3-4
Whenever I am afraid, I will trust in You. In God (I will praise His word), in God I have put my trust; I will not fear. What can flesh do to me?

Psalm 56:11
In God I have put my trust; I will not be afraid. What can man do to me?

25. I Am Not Afraid; My God Is Leading Me Safely
Psalm 78:53
And He led them on safely, so that they did not fear; but the sea overwhelmed their enemies.

26. God Is My Protection
Psalm 91:3,9-10,13-16
Surely He shall deliver you from the snare of the fowler and from the perilous pestilence. 9 Because you have made the Lord, who is my refuge, even the Most High, your dwelling place, 10 no evil shall befall you, nor shall any plague come near your dwelling. 13 You shall tread upon the lion and the cobra, the young lion and the

serpent you shall trample underfoot. 14 "Because he has set his love upon Me, therefore I will deliver him; I will set him on high, because he has known My name. 15 He shall call upon Me, and I will answer him; I will be with him in trouble; I will deliver him and honor him. 16 With long life I will satisfy him, and show him My salvation."

27. **I Am Not Afraid Of Evil Tidings**
Psalm 112:7-8
He will not be afraid of evil tidings; his heart is steadfast, trusting in the Lord. 8 His heart is established; he will not be afraid, until he sees his desire upon his enemies. What can man do to me?

28. **I Am Not Afraid Of Man**
Psalm 118:6
The Lord is on my side; I will not fear. What can man do to me?

29. **My Help Comes From God**
Psalm 121:1-8
I will lift up my eyes to the hills—from whence comes my help? 2 My help comes from the Lord, who made heaven and earth. 3 He will not allow your foot to be moved; He who keeps you will not slumber. 4 Behold, He who keeps Israel shall neither slumber nor sleep. 5 The Lord is your keeper; the Lord is your shade at your right hand. 6 The sun shall not strike you by day, nor the moon by night. 7 The Lord shall preserve you from all evil; He shall preserve your soul. 8 The Lord shall preserve your going out and your coming in from this time forth, and even forevermore.

30. **I Am Not Afraid When I Sleep**
Proverbs 3:24

When you lie down, you will not be afraid; yes, you will lie down and your sleep will be sweet.

31. **I Am Not Afraid Of Sudden Terror**
Proverbs 3:25
Do not be afraid of sudden terror, nor of trouble from the wicked when it comes.

Psalm 91: 5-6
You shall not be afraid of the terror by night, nor of the arrow that flies by day, 6 nor of the pestilence that walks in darkness, nor of the destruction that lays waste at noonday.

32. **The Lord Is A Strong Tower For Me**
Proverbs 18:10
The name of the Lord is a strong tower; the righteous run to it and are safe.

Psalm 61:3
For You have been a shelter for me, a strong tower from the enemy.

33. **I Am Not Afraid, But I Am Strong**
Isaiah 35:4
Say to those who are fearful-hearted, "Be strong, do not fear! Behold, your God will come with vengeance, with the recompense of God; He will come and save you."

Isaiah 41:10
Fear not, for I am with you; be not dismayed, for I am your God. I will strengthen you, yes, I will help you, I will uphold you with My righteous right hand.

34. **I Am Not Afraid, For I Am The Lord's**
Isaiah 43:1-2

But now, thus says the Lord, who created you, O Jacob, and He who formed you, O Israel: "Fear not, for I have redeemed you; I have called you by your name; You are Mine. 2 When you pass through the waters, I will be with you; and through the rivers, they shall not overflow you. When you walk through the fire, you shall not be burned, nor shall the flame scorch you.

35. I Am Not Afraid, I Will Not Be Put To Shame
Isaiah 54:4
Do not fear, for you will not be ashamed neither be disgraced, for you will not be put to shame; for you will forget the shame of your youth, and will not remember the reproach of your widowhood anymore.

36. I Am Far From Oppression, And I Am Not Afraid
Isaiah 54:14
In righteousness you shall be established; you shall be far from oppression, for you shall not fear; and from terror, for it shall not come near you.

37. No Weapon Formed Against Me Shall Prosper
Isaiah 54:17
No weapon formed against you shall prosper, and every tongue which rises against you in judgment you shall condemn. This is the heritage of the servants of the Lord, and their righteousness is from Me, says the Lord.

38. I Am Not Afraid Of Man
Jeremiah 1:8
Do not be afraid of their faces, for I am with you to deliver you, says the Lord.

Jeremiah 1:17
Therefore prepare yourself and arise, and speak to them all that I command you. Do not be dismayed before their

faces, lest I dismay you before them.

Isaiah 51:12
I, even I, am He who comforts you. Who are you that you should be afraid of a man who will die, and of the son of a man who will be made like grass?

39. I Am Not Afraid
Zephaniah 3:16-17
In that day it shall be said to Jerusalem: "Do not fear; Zion, let not your hands be weak. 17 The Lord your God in your midst, The Mighty One, will save; He will rejoice over you with gladness, He will quiet you with His love, He will rejoice over you with singing."

40. I Do Not Fear My Enemies; I Fear God
Matthew 10:26
Therefore do not fear them. For there is nothing covered that will not be revealed, and hidden that will not be known.

Matthew 10:28
And do not fear those who kill the body but cannot kill the soul. But rather fear Him who is able to destroy both soul and body in hell.

41. I Am Not Afraid Of Not Having Enough; I Am Valuable To God
Matthew 10:31
Do not fear therefore; you are of more value than many sparrows.

Luke 12:7
But the very hairs of your head are all numbered. Do not fear therefore; you are of more value than many sparrows.

42. I Am Not Afraid Of Rumors Of Wars
Matthew 24:4-6

And Jesus answered and said to them: "Take heed that no one deceives you. 5 For many will come in My name, saying, 'I am the Christ,' and will deceive many. 6 And you will hear of wars and rumors of wars. See that you are not troubled; for all these things must come to pass, but the end is not yet".

43. I Am Not Afraid When I Encounter God's Angels
Matthew 28:4-5

And the guards shook for fear of him, and became like dead men. 5 But the angel answered and said to the women, "Do not be afraid, for I know that you seek Jesus who was crucified".

Luke 2:9-10

And behold, an angel of the Lord stood before them, and the glory of the Lord shone around them, and they were greatly afraid. 10 Then the angel said to them, "Do not be afraid, for behold, I bring you good tidings of great joy which will be to all people".

44. I Am Not Afraid Because I Have Authority Over The Devil
Matthew 28:18-19

And Jesus came and spoke to them, saying, "All authority has been given to Me in heaven and on earth. 19 Go therefore and make disciples of all the nations, baptizing them in the name of the Father and of the Son and of the Holy Spirit".

45. I Am Not Afraid To Believe God
Mark 5:36

As soon as Jesus heard the word that was spoken, He said to the ruler of the synagogue, "Do not be afraid; only believe."

Luke 8:50
But when Jesus heard it, He answered him, saying, "Do not be afraid; only believe, and she will be made well."

46. I Am Not Afraid Of God's Angels
Luke 1:12-13
And when Zacharias saw him, he was troubled, and fear fell upon him. 13 But the angel said to him, "Do not be afraid, Zacharias, for your prayer is heard; and your wife Elizabeth will bear you a son, and you shall call his name John".

Luke 1:30
Then the angel said to her, "Do not be afraid, Mary, for you have found favor with God".

47. I Am Not Afraid, For Nothing Shall Hurt Me
Luke 10:19
Behold, I give you power to tread on serpents and scorpions, and over all the power of the enemy; and nothing shall by any means hurt you.

48. I Am Not Afraid Of Man; But I Have A Godly Fear
Luke 12:4-5
And I say to you, My friends, do not be afraid of those who kill the body, and after that have no more that they can do. 5 But I will show you whom you should fear: Fear Him who, after He has killed, has power to cast into hell; yes, I say to you, fear Him!

49. I Am Not Afraid, For My Father Gives Me The Kingdom
Luke 12:32
Do not fear, little flock, for it is your Father's good

pleasure to give you the kingdom.

50. I Will Not Be Afraid
John 14:27
Peace I leave with you, My peace I give to you; not as the world gives do I give to you. Let not your heart be troubled, neither let it be afraid.

Psalm 9:9
The Lord also will be a refuge for the oppressed, a refuge in times of trouble.

51. I Am Kept By God From Evil
John 17:15
I do not pray that You should take them out of the world, but that You should keep them from the evil one.

52. I Am Not Afraid To Speak
Acts 18:9-10
Now the Lord spoke to Paul in the night by a vision, "Do not be afraid, but speak, and do not keep silent; 10 for I am with you, and no one will attack you to hurt you; for I have many people in this city."

53. God Is For Me, Nothing Triumphs Over Me
Romans 8:31, 33-35, 38, 39
What then shall we say to these things? If God is for us, who can be against us? 33 Who shall bring a charge against God's elect? It is God who justifies. 34 Who is he who condemns? 35 Who shall separate us from the love of Christ? Shall tribulation, or distress, or persecution, or famine, or nakedness, or peril, or sword? 38 For I am persuaded that neither death nor life, nor angels nor principalities nor powers, nor things present nor things to come, 39 nor height nor depth, nor any other created thing, shall be able to separate us from the love of God

which is in Christ Jesus our Lord.

54. I Am Not Afraid, For God Has Crushed Satan
Romans 16:20
And the God of peace will crush Satan under your feet shortly. The grace of our Lord Jesus Christ be with you. Amen.

55. I Am Not Afraid; I Take Every Thought Captive
2 Corinthians 10:3-5
For though we walk n the flesh, we do not war according to the flesh. 4 For the weapons of our warfare are not carnal but mighty in God for pulling down strongholds, 5 casting down arguments and every high thing that exalts itself against the knowledge of God, bringing every thought into captivity to the obedience of Christ.

56. I Have No Fear; Only Confidence
Philippians 1:6
...being confident of this very thing, that He who has begun a good work in you will complete it until the day of Jesus Christ.

57. Jesus Has Already Defeated The Devil
Colossians 2:15
...having disarmed principalities and powers, He made a public spectacle of them, triumphing over them in it.

58. God Has Given Me A Spirit Of Power, Love, And A Sound Mind
2 Timothy 1:7
For God has not given us a spirit of fear, but of power and of love and of a sound mind.

Romans 8:15
For you did not receive the spirit of bondage again to

fear, but you received the Spirit of adoption by whom we cry out, "Abba, Father."

59. **He Will Protect Me From The Evil One**
2 Thessalonians 3:3
But the Lord is faithful, who will establish you and guard you from the evil one.

60. **He Will Never Leave Or Forsake Me**
Hebrews 13:5
Let your conduct be without covetousness; be content with such things as you have. For He Himself has said, "I will never leave you nor forsake you."

61. **The Lord Is My Helper; I Will Not Fear Man**
Hebrews 13:6
So we may boldly say: "The Lord is my helper; I will not fear. What can man do to me?"

1 Peter 3:14
But even if you should suffer for righteousness' sake, you are blessed. "And do not be afraid of their threats, nor be troubled."

62. **I Do Not Fear The Devil; I Resist The Devil And He Flees From Me In Terror**
James 4:7
Therefore submit to God. Resist the devil and he will flee from you.

63. **God's Perfect Love For Me Casts Out Any Fear**
1 John 4:18
There is no fear in love; but perfect love casts out fear, because fear involves torment.

64. I Am Not Afraid To See Jesus
Revelation 1:17
And when I saw Him, I fell at His feet as dead. But He laid His right hand on me, saying to me, "Do not be afraid; I am the First and the Last.

Matthew 14:27
But immediately Jesus spoke to them, saying, "Be of good cheer! It is I; do not be afraid."

Matthew 17:7
But Jesus came and touched them and said, "Arise, and do not be afraid."

Matthew 28:10
Then Jesus said to them, "Do not be afraid. Go *and* tell My brethren to go to Galilee, and there they will see Me."

Mark 6:50
...for they all saw Him and were troubled. But immediately He talked with them and said to them, "Be of good cheer! It is I; do not be afraid."

John 6:20
But He said to them, "It is I; do not be afraid."

65. I Will Not Fear In Tribulation
Revelation 2:10
Do not fear any of those things which you are about to suffer. Indeed, the devil is about to throw some of you into prison, that you may be tested, and you will have tribulation ten days. Be faithful until death, and I will give you the crown of life.

CHAPTER SEVEN

Salvation

2 Peter 3:9
The Lord is ... not willing that any should perish but that all should come to repentance.

1 Timothy 2:4
...who desires all men to be saved and to come to the knowledge of the truth.

The Gospel of John has much to say about the subject of salvation. Jesus came to bridge the gap between man and God. He is the way to the Father. He says in His Word that anyone who comes to Him, He will not cast out. It is God's will for everyone to be saved. Some, however, may refuse the invitation. But, we are still His only witnesses on the earth, so we are the ones to share the good news with those who are perishing. (The eight **I AM Scriptures** are written in bold intentionally).

Ask yourself the following questions, as you read the scriptures on salvation.

1. What is the way to the Father?
2. What is God's will concerning salvation?
3. Why did Jesus come?
4. Who can be saved?
5. What is our part in the great commission?

CHAPTER SEVEN

Salvation

1. God, You Are Faithful To Keep My Family Line
Deuteronomy 7:9
Therefore know that the Lord your God, He is God, the faithful God who keeps covenant and mercy for a thousand generations with those who love Him and keep His commandments.

2. I Ask You For The Nations As My Inheritance
Psalm 2:8
Ask of Me, and I will give You the nations for Your inheritance, and the ends of the earth for Your possession.

3. I Win Souls And I Am Wise
Proverbs 11:30
The fruit of the righteous is a tree of life, and he who wins souls is wise.

4. My Children Will Not Depart From The Lord
Proverbs 22:6
Train up a child in the way he should go, and when he is old he will not depart from it.

5. Only The Lord Can Wash Away Sin
Isaiah 1:18
Come now, and let us reason together," says the Lord, "Though your sins are like scarlet, they shall be as white as snow; though they are red like crimson, they shall be as wool.

6. God Is Bringing My Children Home
Isaiah 43:5-6
Fear not, for I am with you; I will bring your descendants from the east, and gather you from the west. 6 I will say to the north, 'Give them up!' And to the south, 'Do not keep them back!' Bring My sons from afar, and My daughters from the ends of the earth.

Isaiah 60:4
Lift up your eyes all around, and see: They all gather together, they come to you; your sons shall come from afar, and your daughters shall be nursed at *your* side.

Jeremiah 30:10
'Therefore do not fear, O My servant Jacob,' says the LORD, 'Nor be dismayed, O Israel; for behold, I will save you from afar, and your seed from the land of their captivity. Jacob shall return, have rest and be quiet, and no one shall make *him* afraid. 11 For I *am* with you,' says the LORD, 'to save you'.

7. When He Forgives Me, He Remembers My Sins No More
Isaiah 43:25-26
I, even I, am He who blots out your transgressions for My own sake; and I will not remember your sins. 26 Put Me in remembrance; let us contend together; state your case, that you may be acquitted.

Isaiah 44:22
I have blotted out, like a thick cloud, your transgressions, and like a cloud, your sins. Return to Me, for I have redeemed you.

Psalm 103:12
As far as the east is from the west, so far has He removed our transgressions from us.

8. God Will Pour His Spirit On My Descendants
Isaiah 44:3
For I will pour water on him who is thirsty, and floods on the dry ground; I will pour My Spirit on your descendants, and My blessing on your offspring.

9. God Doesn't Hear Us When There Is Iniquity In Us
Isaiah 59:1-2
Behold, the Lord's hand is not shortened, that it cannot save; nor His ear heavy, that it cannot hear. 2 But your iniquities have separated you from your God; and your sins have hidden His face from you, so that He will not hear.

10. God Is Willing To Forgive Us
Jeremiah 33:8
I will cleanse them from all their iniquity by which they have sinned against Me, and I will pardon all their iniquities by which they have sinned and by which they have transgressed against Me.

11. Let Us Warn The Wicked
Ezekiel 3:18-21
When I say to the wicked, 'You shall surely die,' and you give him no warning, nor speak to warn the wicked from his wicked way, to save his life, that same wicked man shall die in his iniquity; but his blood I will require at your hand. 19 Yet, if you warn the wicked, and he does not turn from his wickedness, nor from his wicked way, he

shall die in his iniquity; but you have delivered your soul. 20 "Again, when a righteous man turns from his righteousness and commits iniquity, and I lay a stumbling block before him, he shall die; because you did not give him warning, he shall die in his sin, and his righteousness which he has done shall not be remembered; but his blood I will require at your hand. 21 Nevertheless if you warn the righteous man that the righteous should not sin, and he does not sin, he shall surely live because he took warning; also you will have delivered your soul."

12. **God Wants The Wicked To Repent And Live**
Ezekiel 18:23
"Do I have any pleasure at all that the wicked should die?" says the Lord God, "and not that he should turn from his ways and live"?

Ezekiel 33:11
Say to them: 'As I live,' says the Lord God, 'I have no pleasure in the death of the wicked, but that the wicked turn from his way and live. Turn, turn from your evil ways! For why should you die, O house of Israel?'

13. **The Lord God Seeks The Lost**
Ezekiel 34:11-12,16
'For thus says the Lord God: "Indeed I Myself will search for My sheep and seek them out. 12 As a shepherd seeks out his flock on the day he is among his scattered sheep, so will I seek out My sheep and deliver them from all the places where they were scattered on a cloudy and dark day. 16 "I will seek what was lost and bring back what was driven away, bind up the broken and strengthen what was sick; but I will destroy the fat and the strong, and feed them in judgment."

14. Jesus Came To Save Mankind
Matthew 1:21
And she will bring forth a Son, and you shall call His name Jesus, for He will save His people from their sins.

15. I Am A Fisher Of Men
Matthew 4:19
Then He said to them, "Follow Me, and I will make you fishers of men."

16. I Pray For Laborers Into The Harvest Fields
Matthew 9:37-38
Then He said to His disciples, "The harvest truly is plentiful, but the laborers are few. 38 Therefore pray the Lord of the harvest to send out laborers into His harvest."

17. I Confess Jesus As My Lord
Matthew 10:32
Therefore whoever confesses Me before men, him I will also confess before My Father who is in heaven.

18. There Is No Profit For A Man Who Gains The Whole World But Loses His Soul
Matthew 16:25-28
For whoever desires to save his life will lose it, but whoever loses his life for My sake will find it. 26 For what profit is it to a man if he gains the whole world, and loses his own soul? Or what will a man give in exchange for his soul? 27 For the Son of Man will come in the glory of His Father with His angels, and then He will reward each according to his works. 28 "Assuredly, I say to you, there are some standing here who shall not taste death till they see the Son of Man coming in His kingdom."

19. **We Enter The Kingdom Of God As A Child**
Matthew 18:3
And said, assuredly, I say to you, unless you are converted and become as little children, you will by no means enter the kingdom of heaven.

20. **God's Will Is That None Perish**
Matthew 18:12-14
What do you think? If a man has a hundred sheep, and one of them goes astray, does he not leave the ninety-nine and go to the mountains to seek the one that is straying? 13 And if he should find it, assuredly, I say to you, he rejoices more over that sheep than over the ninety-nine that did not go astray. 14 Even so it is not the will of your Father who is in heaven that one of these little ones should perish.

1 Timothy 2:3-4
For this is good and acceptable in the sight of God our Savior, 4 who desires all men to be saved and to come to the knowledge of the truth.

21. **I Pray That Their Hearts Are Not Dull So They Can See**
Mark 4:12
'Seeing they may see and not perceive, and hearing they may hear and not understand; lest they should turn, and their sins be forgiven them.'"

Matthew 13:14-17
'Hearing you will hear and shall not understand, and seeing you will see and not perceive; 15 For the hearts of this people have grown dull. Their ears are hard of hearing, and their eyes they have closed, lest they should

see with their eyes and hear with their ears, lest they should understand with their hearts and turn, so that I should heal them.' 16 But blessed are your eyes for they see, and your ears for they hear; 17 for assuredly, I say to you that many prophets and righteous men desired to see what you see, and did not see it, and to hear what you hear, and did not hear it.

Isaiah 6:10
"Make the heart of this people dull, and their ears heavy, and shut their eyes; lest they see with their eyes, and hear with their ears, and understand with their heart, and return and be healed."

22. **The Righteous Will Be Saved**
Matthew 25:46
And these will go away into everlasting punishment, but the righteous into eternal life.

Mark 16:15-16
And He said to them, "Go into all the world and preach the gospel to every creature. 16 He who believes and is baptized will be saved; but he who does not believe will be condemned".

23. **Jesus Came For Sinners, To Save The Lost**
Luke 5:32
I have not come to call the righteous, but sinners, to repentance.

Matthew 1:21
And she will bring forth a Son, and you shall call His name Jesus, for He will save His people from their sins.

Luke 19:10

...for the Son of Man has come to seek and to save that which was lost.

24. **There Is Rejoicing Over One Sinner Who Repents**
(Parable Of The Lost Sheep)
Luke 15:4-7

"What man of you, having a hundred sheep, if he loses one of them, does not leave the ninety-nine in the wilderness, and go after the one which is lost until he finds it? 5 And when he has found it, he lays it on his shoulders, rejoicing. 6 And when he comes home, he calls together his friends and neighbors, saying to them, 'Rejoice with me, for I have found my sheep which was lost!' 7 I say to you that likewise there will be more joy in heaven over one sinner who repents than over ninety-nine just persons who need no repentance".

(Parable Of The Lost Coin)
Luke 15:9-10

And when she has found it, she calls her friends and neighbors together, saying, 'Rejoice with me, for I have found the piece which I lost!' 10 Likewise, I say to you, there is joy in the presence of the angels of God over one sinner who repents."

25. **There Is Rejoicing When The Lost Is Found**
(Parable Of The Lost Son)
Luke 15:23-24,32

'And bring the fatted calf here and kill it, and let us eat and be merry; 24 for this my son was dead and is alive again; he was lost and is found.' And they began to be merry. 32 It was right that we should make merry and be glad, for your brother was dead and is alive again, and was lost and is found.'"

26. When Eyes Are Open They Can See Jesus
Luke 24:31,45

Then their eyes were opened and they knew Him; and He vanished from their sight. 45 And He opened their understanding, that they might comprehend the Scriptures.

27. Whoever Receives Jesus Is A Child Of God
John 1:7-13

This man came for a witness, to bear witness of the Light, that all through him might believe. 8 He was not that Light, but was sent to bear witness of that Light. 9 That was the true Light which gives light to every man coming into the world. 10 He was in the world, and the world was made through Him, and the world did not know Him. 11 He came to His own, and His own did not receive Him. 12 But as many as received Him, to them He gave the right to become children of God, to those who believe in His name: 13 who were born, not of blood, nor of the will of the flesh, nor of the will of man, but of God.

28. Your Spirit Must Be Born Again
John 3:1-7

There was a man of the Pharisees named Nicodemus, a ruler of the Jews. 2 This man came to Jesus by night and said to Him, "Rabbi, we know that You are a teacher come from God; for no one can do these signs that You do unless God is with him." 3 Jesus answered and said to him, "Most assuredly, I say to you, unless one is born again, he cannot see the kingdom of God." 4 Nicodemus said to Him, "How can a man be born when he is old? Can he enter a second time into his mother's womb and be born?" 5 Jesus answered, "Most assuredly, I say to you, unless one is born of water and the Spirit, he cannot enter the kingdom of God. 6 That which is born of the flesh is flesh, and that which is born of the Spirit is spirit. 7 Do not marvel that I said to you, 'You must be born again'.

29. **Jesus Came To Save The World**
John 3:16-17
 For God so loved the world that He gave His only begotten Son, that whoever believes in Him should not perish but have everlasting life. 17 For God did not send His Son into the world to condemn the world, but that the world through Him might be saved.

30. **Whoever Believes In Jesus Has Everlasting Life**
John 3:18, 36
He who believes in Him is not condemned; but he who does not believe is condemned already, because he has not believed in the name of the only begotten Son of God. 36 He who believes in the Son has everlasting life; and he who does not believe the Son shall not see life, but the wrath of God abides on him."

John 4:14
 "But whoever drinks of the water that I shall give him will never thirst. But the water that I shall give him will become in him a fountain of water springing up into everlasting life."

31. **Everlasting Life Comes Through Believing In Jesus**
John 5:21, 24-29, 34, 38-40
 For as the Father raises the dead and gives life to them, even so the Son gives life to whom He will. 24 "Most assuredly, I say to you, he who hears My word and

believes in Him who sent Me has everlasting life, and shall not come into judgment, but has passed from death into life. 25 Most assuredly, I say to you, the hour is coming, and now is, when the dead will hear the voice of the Son of God; and those who hear will live. 26 For as the Father has life in Himself, so He has granted the Son to have life in Himself, 27 and has given Him authority to execute judgment also, because He is the Son of Man. 28 Do not marvel at this; for the hour is coming in which all who are in the graves will hear His voice 29 and come forth—those who have done good, to the resurrection of life, and those who have done evil, to the resurrection of condemnation. 34 Yet I do not receive testimony from man, but I say these things that you may be saved. 38 But you do not have His word abiding in you, because whom He sent, Him you do not believe. 39 You search the Scriptures, for in them you think you have eternal life; and these are they which testify of Me. 40 But you are not willing to come to Me that you may have life".

32. Whoever Believes In Jesus Shall Never Hunger Or Thirst
John 6:35, 48, 51

And Jesus said to them, "I am the bread of life. He who comes to Me shall never hunger, and he who believes in Me shall never thirst. 48 I am the bread of life. 51 I am the living bread which came down from heaven. If anyone eats of this bread, he will live forever; and the bread that I shall give is My flesh, which I shall give for the life of the world." **(I AM Scripture)**

33. Whoever Believes In Jesus Has Everlasting Life
John 6:40, 47

"And this is the will of Him who sent Me, that everyone who sees the Son and believes in Him may have everlasting life; and I will raise him up at the last day." 47 Most assuredly, I say to you, he who believes in Me has everlasting life.

34. **Jesus Is The Light Of The World**
John 8:12
Then Jesus spoke to them again, saying**, "I am the light of the world.** He who follows Me shall not walk in darkness, but have the light of life."

John 9:5
"As long as I am in the world, **I am the light of the world." (I AM Scripture)**

35. **Before Abraham There Was Jesus**
John 8:58
Jesus said to them, **"Most assuredly, I say to you, before Abraham was, I AM." (I AM Scripture)**

36. **Jesus Is The Door To Salvation**
John 10: 7,9
Then Jesus said to them again**, "Most assuredly, I say to you, I am the door of the sheep. 9 I am the door. If anyone enters by Me, he will be saved, and will go in and out and find pasture". (I AM Scripture)**

37. **Jesus Is The Good Shepherd**
John 10:10-11,14,15
I have come that they may have life, and that they may have it more abundantly. 11**"I am the good shepherd. The good shepherd gives His life for the sheep. 14 I am the good shepherd; and I know My sheep, and am known by My own.** 15 As the Father knows Me, even so I know the Father; and I lay down My life for the sheep". **(I AM Scripture**)

38. Jesus Is The Resurrection And The Life
John 11:25
Jesus said to her, **"I am the resurrection and the life. He who believes in Me, though he may die, he shall live". (I AM Scripture)**

39. Whoever Believes In Jesus Believes In Father God Who Sent Him
John 12:36, 44-50
While you have the light, believe in the light, that you may become sons of light. 44 Then Jesus cried out and said, "He who believes in Me, believes not in Me but in Him who sent Me. 45 And he who sees Me sees Him who sent Me. 46 I have come as a light into the world, that whoever believes in Me should not abide in darkness. 47 And if anyone hears My words and does not believe, I do not judge him; for I did not come to judge the world but to save the world. 48 He who rejects Me, and does not receive My words, has that which judges him—the word that I have spoken will judge him in the last day. 49 For I have not spoken on My own authority; but the Father who sent Me gave Me a command, what I should say and what I should speak. 50 And I know that His command is everlasting life. Therefore, whatever I speak, just as the Father has told Me, so I speak."

40. Jesus Is The Way, The Truth, And The Life
John 14:1-6
"Let not your heart be troubled; you believe in God, believe also in Me. 2 In My Father's house are many mansions; if it were not so, I would have told you. I go to prepare a place for you. 3 And if I go and prepare a place for you, I will come again and receive you to Myself; that where I am, there you may be also. 4 And where I go you

know, and the way you know." 5 Thomas said to Him, "Lord, we do not know where You are going, and how can we know the way?" **6 Jesus said to him, "I am the way, the truth, and the life. No one comes to the Father except through Me"'. (I AM Scripture)**

41. Jesus Is The True Vine
John 15:1,5
"I am the true vine, and My Father is the vinedresser". 5 "I am the vine, you are the branches. He who abides in Me, and I in him, bears much fruit; for without Me you can do nothing". **(I AM Scripture)**

42. The Holy Spirit Convicts The World Of Sin
John 16:7-8
Nevertheless I tell you the truth. It is to your advantage that I go away; for if I do not go away, the Helper will not come to you; but if I depart, I will send Him to you. 8 And when He has come, He will convict the world of sin, and of righteousness, and of judgment.

43. Eternal Life Is Knowing God Through Jesus Christ
John 17:1-3, 11-12, 20-21
Jesus spoke these words, lifted up His eyes to heaven, and said: "Father, the hour has come. Glorify Your Son, that Your Son also may glorify You, 2 as You have given Him authority over all flesh, that He should give eternal life to as many as You have given Him. 3 And this is eternal life, that they may know You, the only true God, and Jesus Christ whom You have sent. 11 Holy Father, keep through Your name those whom You have given Me, that they may be one as We are. 12 While I was with them in the world, I kept them in Your name.

Those whom You gave Me I have kept; and none of them is lost except the son of perdition, that the Scripture might be fulfilled. 20 "I do not pray for these alone, but also for those who will believe in Me through their word; 21 that they all may be one, as You, Father, are in Me, and I in You; that they also may be one in Us, that the world may believe that You sent Me".

John 20:29-31
Jesus said to him, "Thomas, because you have seen Me, you have believed. Blessed are those who have not seen and yet have believed." 30 And truly Jesus did many other signs in the presence of His disciples, which are not written in this book; 31 but these are written that you may believe that Jesus is the Christ, the Son of God, and that believing you may have life in His name.

44. **Anyone Who Calls On The Name Of Jesus Shall Be Saved**
Acts 2:21
And it shall come to pass that whoever calls on the name of the Lord shall be saved.

Acts 2:38, 47
Then Peter said to them, "Repent, and let every one of you be baptized in the name of Jesus Christ for the remission of sins; and you shall receive the gift of the Holy Spirit". 47 And the Lord added to the church daily those who were being saved.

Acts 3:19
Repent therefore and be converted, that your sins may be blotted out, so that times of refreshing may come from the presence of the Lord.

Acts 10:43
To Him all the prophets witness that, through His name, whoever believes in Him will receive remission of sins.

Acts 14:1
Now it happened in Iconium that they went together to the synagogue of the Jews, and so spoke that a great multitude both of the Jews and of the Greeks believed.

45. **There Is No Other Name By Which Men Shall Be Saved**
Acts 4:12
Nor is there salvation in any other, for there is no other name under heaven given among men by which we must be saved.

Acts 11:17-18
"If therefore God gave them the same gift as He gave us when we believed on the Lord Jesus Christ, who was I that I could withstand God?" 18 When they heard these things they became silent; and they glorified God, saying, "Then God has also granted to the Gentiles repentance to life."

Acts 13:38-39
Therefore let it be known to you, brethren, that through this Man is preached to you the forgiveness of sins; 39 and by Him everyone who believes is justified from all things from which you could not be justified by the law of Moses.

46. **I Am Worthy Of Everlasting Life**
Acts 13:46-48
Then Paul and Barnabas grew bold and said, "It was necessary that the word of God should be spoken to you

first; but since you reject it, and judge yourselves unworthy of everlasting life, behold, we turn to the Gentiles. 47 For so the Lord has commanded us: 'I have set you as a light to the Gentiles, that you should be for salvation to the ends of the earth.'" 48 Now when the Gentiles heard this, they were glad and glorified the word of the Lord. And as many as had been appointed to eternal life believed.

47. **Believe In Jesus And Your Household Will Be Saved**
Acts 16:31
So they said, "Believe on the Lord Jesus Christ, and you will be saved, you and your household."

Acts 11:14
Who will tell you words by which you and all your household will be saved.

48. **God Calls His Children As His Mouthpiece To Try To Persuade Men**
Acts 26:17-18, 28-29
'I will deliver you from the Jewish people, as well as from the Gentiles, to whom I now send you, 18 to open their eyes, in order to turn them from darkness to light, and from the power of Satan to God, that they may receive forgiveness of sins and an inheritance among those who are sanctified by faith in Me.'

Acts 26:28-29
Then Agrippa said to Paul, "You almost persuade me to become a Christian." 29 And Paul said, "I would to God that not only you, but also all who hear me today, might become both almost and altogether such as I am, except for these chains."

49. The Gospel Is The Power Of God To Salvation
Romans 1:16-17

For I am not ashamed of the gospel of Christ, for it is the power of God to salvation for everyone who believes, for the Jew first and also for the Greek. 17 For in it the righteousness of God is revealed from faith to faith; as it is written, "The just shall live by faith."

50. All Have Sinned And Fall Short Of The Glory Of God
Romans 3:22-24

Even the righteousness of God, through faith in Jesus Christ, to all and on all who believe. For there is no difference; 23 for all have sinned and fall short of the glory of God, 24 being justified freely by His grace through the redemption that is in Christ Jesus.

51. While We Were Sinners Christ Died For Us
Romans 5:8-9

But God demonstrates His own love toward us, in that while we were still sinners, Christ died for us. 9 Much more then, having now been justified by His blood, we shall be saved from wrath through Him.

52. The Gift Of God Is Eternal Life
Romans 6:22-23

But now having been set free from sin, and having become slaves of God, you have your fruit to holiness, and the end, everlasting life. 23 For the wages of sin is death, but the gift of God is eternal life in Christ Jesus our Lord.

53. If You Confess And Believe In Jesus, You Will Be Saved
Romans 10:9-10

That if you confess with your mouth the Lord Jesus and believe in your heart that God has raised Him from the dead, you will be saved. 10 For with the heart one believes unto righteousness, and with the mouth confession is made unto salvation.

54. **The Unbelieving Husband Is Sanctified By His Believing Wife**
1 Corinthians 7:13-16
And a woman who has a husband who does not believe, if he is willing to live with her, let her not divorce him. 14 For the unbelieving husband is sanctified by the wife, and the unbelieving wife is sanctified by the husband; otherwise your children would be unclean, but now they are holy. 15 But if the unbeliever departs, let him depart; a brother or a sister is not under bondage in such cases. But God has called us to peace. 16 For how do you know, O wife, whether you will save your husband? Or how do you know, O husband, whether you will save your wife?

1 Peter 3:1-2
Wives, likewise, be submissive to your own husbands, that even if some do not obey the word, they, without a word, may be won by the conduct of their wives, 2 when they observe your chaste conduct accompanied by fear.

55. **The Gospel Is Veiled To The Perishing Until They See The Light**
2 Corinthians 4:3
But even if our gospel is veiled, it is veiled to those who are perishing, 4 whose minds the god of this age has blinded, who do not believe, lest the light of the gospel of the glory of Christ, who is the image of God, should shine on them.

56. **Anyone Who Is Born Again Is A New Creation**
2 Corinthians 5:17

Therefore, if anyone is in Christ, he is a new creation; old things have passed away; behold, all things have become new.

57. **Today Is The Day Of Salvation**
2 Corinthians 6:2

For He says: "In an acceptable time I have heard you, and in the day of salvation I have helped you. Behold, now is the accepted time; behold, now is the day of salvation".

58. **Whoever Sows To The Spirit Will Reap Eternal Life**
Galatians 6:8

For he who sows to his flesh will of the flesh reap corruption, but he who sows to the Spirit will of the Spirit reap everlasting life.

59. **We Are Saved By Grace Through Faith**
Ephesians 2:1, 4-5,8-9

And you He made alive, who were dead in trespasses and sins, 4 But God, who is rich in mercy, because of His great love with which He loved us, 5 even when we were dead in trespasses, made us alive together with Christ (by grace you have been saved), 8 For by grace you have been saved through faith, and that not of yourselves; it is the gift of God, 9 not of works, lest anyone should boast.

Acts 15:11
But we believe that through the grace of the Lord Jesus Christ we shall be saved in the same manner as they.

60. Jesus Delivered Us Out Of Darkness And Into The Light
Colossians 1:13-14, 21
He has delivered us from the power of darkness and conveyed us into the kingdom of the Son of His love, 14 in whom we have redemption through His blood, the forgiveness of sins. 21 And you, who once were alienated and enemies in your mind by wicked works, yet now He has reconciled.

61. If You Correct With Humility, God Will Grant Repentance And They Can Come To Their Senses
2 Timothy 2: 25-26
In humility correcting those who are in opposition, if God perhaps will grant them repentance, so that they may know the truth, 26 and that they may come to their senses and escape the snare of the devil, having been taken captive by him to do his will.

62. He Saved Us By His Mercy
Titus 3:5
Not by works of righteousness which we have done, but according to His mercy He saved us, through the washing of regeneration and renewing.

63. He Who Saves A Soul Covers A Multitude Of Sins
James 5:20
Let him know that he who turns a sinner from the error of his way will save a soul from death and cover a multitude of sins.

64. I Do Not Draw Back But Believe
Hebrews 10:38-39
Now the just shall live by faith; but if anyone draws back, My soul has no pleasure in him.

65. **God Is Not Willing For Any To Perish**
2 Peter 3:9
The Lord is not slack concerning His promise, as some count slackness, but is longsuffering toward us, not willing that any should perish but that all should come to repentance.

1 Timothy 2:1-4
Therefore I exhort first of all that supplications, prayers, intercessions, *and* giving of thanks be made for all men, 2 for kings and all who are in authority, that we may lead a quiet and peaceable life in all godliness and reverence. 3 For this *is* good and acceptable in the sight of God our Savior, 4 who desires all men to be saved and to come to the knowledge of the truth.

CHAPTER EIGHT

Deliverance

Psalm 34:7
The angel of the Lord encamps all around those who fear Him, and delivers them.

David wrote most of the psalms, and there we find many verses on the hope David had for deliverance. God promises us in His word to deliver us from many things - from evil, from our evil desires, from sickness and disease and from trouble, famine, and even from premature death.

We have all, no doubt, heard stories of folks who were delivered from terrible accidents or tragedies. There are many stories of survivors of car crashes, and even terrorist attacks, like during 9/11. God does watch over His children, and delivers them from the works of the enemy. We can trust Him in these dangerous times.

As you consider the truths in this chapter, answer the following questions.
1. Is it Gods will to deliver me?
2. Who will He deliver?
3. How does deliverance come?
4. What does He deliver me out of?
5. Will He deliver me in the coming troubled times?

CHAPTER EIGHT

Deliverance

1. God Is My Rescuer And Deliverer
Exodus 6:6
Therefore say to the children of Israel: 'I am the Lord; I will bring you out from under the burdens of the Egyptians, I will rescue you from their bondage, and I will redeem you with an outstretched arm and with great judgments'.

2. God Delivers Me From My Enemies; He Is My Redeemer
Deuteronomy 28:7
"The Lord will cause your enemies who rise against you to be defeated before your face; they shall come out against you one way and flee before you seven ways".

Job 19:25
For I know that my Redeemer lives, and He shall stand at last on the earth.

Job 33:28
He will redeem his soul from going down to the pit, and his life shall see the ight.

3. God Delivers Out Of Bondage
Joshua 24:17
For the Lord our God is He who brought us and our fathers up out of the land of Egypt, from the house of bondage, who did those great signs in our sight, and preserved us in all the way that we went and among all the people through whom we passed.

4. He Delivers The Ones Whom I Pray For
Job 22:30
He will even deliver one who is not innocent; yes, he will be delivered by the purity of your hands.

5. God Is My Deliverer
Psalm 18:2-3,6,17,19,47-48
The Lord is my rock and my fortress and my deliverer; my God, my strength, in whom I will trust; my shield and the horn of my salvation, my stronghold. 3 I will call upon the LORD, *who is worthy* to be praised; so shall I be saved from my enemies. 6 In my distress I called upon the LORD, and cried out to my God; He heard my voice from His temple, and my cry came before Him, *even* to His ears. 17 He delivered me from my strong enemy, from those who hated me, for they were too strong for me. 19 He also brought me out into a broad place; He delivered me because He delighted in me. 47 It is God who avenges me, and subdues the peoples under me; 48 He delivers me from my enemies. You also lift me up above those who rise against me; You have delivered me from the violent man.

6. My God Does Deliver Me!
Psalm 25:20
Keep my soul, and deliver me; let me not be ashamed, for I put my trust in You.

Psalm 6:4
Return, O Lord, deliver me! Oh, save me for Your mercies' sake!

7. You Deliver Me, Oh Lord
Psalm 31:1-2
In You, O Lord, I put my trust; let me never be ashamed; deliver me in Your righteousness. 2 Bow down Your ear

to me; deliver me speedily; be my rock of refuge, a fortress of defense to save me.

8. **My God Surrounds Me With His Deliverance**
Psalm 32:7
You are my hiding place; You shall preserve me from trouble; You shall surround me with songs of deliverance. Selah

9. **My God Delivers Me In Time Of Famine**
Psalm 33:18-19
Behold; the eye of the Lord is on those who fear Him, on those who hope in His mercy, 19 to deliver their soul from death, and to keep them alive in famine.

10. **God Hears Me When I Cry Out To Him And He Delivers Me**
Psalm 34:4,6
I sought the Lord, and He heard me, and delivered me from all my fears. 6 This poor man cried out, and the Lord heard him, and saved him out of all his troubles.

11. **Angels Are Watching Over Me, To Deliver Me**
Psalm 34:7
The angel of the Lord encamps all around those who fear Him, and delivers them.

Psalm 91:11
For He shall give His angels charge over you, to keep you in all your ways.

Matthew 4:6
And said to Him, "If You are the Son of God, throw Yourself down. For it is written: 'He shall give His angels charge over you,' and, 'In their hands they shall bear you up, lest you dash your foot against a stone.'"

Luke 4:10
For it is written: 'He shall give His angels charge over you, to keep you.'

12. God Is My Deliverer
Psalm 34:17-18
The righteous cry out, and the Lord hears, and delivers them out of all their troubles. 18 The Lord is near to those who have a broken heart, and saves such as have a contrite spirit.

13. My God Fights For Me And Delivers Me
Psalm 35:1-3,10
Plead my cause, O Lord, with those who strive with me; fight against those who fight against me. 2 Take hold of shield and buckler, and stand up for my help. 3 Also draw out the spear, and stop those who pursue me. Say to my soul, "I am your salvation." 10 All my bones shall say, "Lord, who is like You, delivering the poor from him who is too strong for him, yes, the poor and the needy from him who plunders him?"

14. My God Delivers Me As I Trust In Him
Psalm 37:17,39-40
For the arms of the wicked shall be broken, But the Lord upholds the righteous. 39 But the salvation of the righteous is from the Lord; He is their strength in the time of trouble. 40 And the Lord shall help them and deliver them; He shall deliver them from the wicked, and save them, because they trust in Him.

15. He Brought Me Up Out Of The Pit
Psalm 40:1-2
I waited patiently for the Lord; and He inclined to me, and heard my cry. 2 He also brought me up out of a horrible

pit, out of the miry clay, and set my feet upon a rock, and established my steps.

16. **He Is My Help And My Deliverer**
Psalm 40:13,17
Be pleased, O Lord, to deliver me; O Lord, make haste to help me! 17 But I am poor and needy; yet the Lord thinks upon me. You are my help and my deliverer; do not delay, O my God.

Psalm 70:1
Make haste, O God, to deliver me! Make haste to help me, O Lord!

17. **He Delivers The Poor**
Psalm 41:1-2
Blessed is he who considers the poor; The Lord will deliver him in time of trouble. 2 The Lord will preserve him and keep him alive, and he will be blessed on the earth; You will not deliver him to the will of his enemies.

Psalm 82:4
Deliver the poor and needy; free them from the hand of the wicked.

18. **When I Call On My God, He Delivers Me**
Psalm 50:15-17
Call upon Me in the day of trouble; I will deliver you, and you shall glorify Me." 16 As for me, I will call upon God, and the LORD shall save me. 17 Evening and morning and at noon I will pray, and cry aloud, and He shall hear my voice.

19. **He Delivers Me Out Of All My Troubles**
Psalm 54:7
For He has delivered me out of all trouble; and my eye

Deliverance

has seen its desire upon my enemies.

20. My God Delivers Me From The Hand Of The Wicked
Psalm 71:2,4
Deliver me in Your righteousness, and cause me to escape; incline Your ear to me, and save me. 4 Deliver me, O my God, out of the hand of the wicked, out of the hand of the unrighteous and cruel man.

Psalm 97:10
You who love the Lord, hate evil! He preserves the souls of His saints; He delivers them out of the hand of the wicked.

21. He Will Deliver Me In Trouble
Psalm 91:3,14-16
 Surely He shall deliver you from the snare of the fowler and from the perilous pestilence. 14 "Because he has set his love upon Me, therefore I will deliver him; I will set him on high, because he has known My name. 15 He shall call upon Me, and I will answer him; I will be with him in trouble; I will deliver him and honor him. 16 With long life I will satisfy him, and show him My salvation."

22. He Redeems Me From My Enemies
Psalm 107:1-3
Oh, give thanks to the Lord, for He is good! For His mercy endures forever. 2 Let the redeemed of the Lord say so, whom He has redeemed from the hand of the enemy, 3 and gathered out of the lands, from the east and from the west, from the north and from the south.

23. He Delivers Me Out Of All My Troubles
Psalm 107:6-7,19-20
Then they cried out to the Lord in their trouble, and He

delivered them out of their distresses. 7 And He led them forth by the right way, that they might go to a city for a dwelling place. 19 Then they cried out to the Lord in their trouble, and He saved them out of their distresses. 20 He sent His word and healed them, and delivered them from their destructions.

Psalm 103:1,4
Bless the Lord, O my soul; 4 who redeems your life from destruction.

24. God Delivers From Death And Darkness
Psalm 107:14
He brought them out of darkness and the shadow of death, and broke their chains in pieces.

25. You Deliver Your Beloved
Psalm 108:5-6
Be exalted, O God, above the heavens, and Your glory above all the earth; 6 that Your beloved may be delivered, save with Your right hand, and hear me.

26. You Deliver My Soul From Death
Psalm 116:8
For You have delivered my soul from death, my eyes from tears, and my feet from falling.

27. Deliver Me According To Your Word
Psalm 119:134,170
Redeem me from the oppression of man, that I may keep Your precepts. 170 Let my supplication come before You; deliver me according to Your word.

28. Deliver Me From Evil Speaking
Psalm 120:2
Deliver my soul, O Lord, from lying lips and from a deceitful tongue.

29. **You Deliver Me From The Snare Of The Fowler**
Psalm 124:7
Our soul has escaped as a bird from the snare of the fowlers; the snare is broken, and we have escaped.

Psalm 91:3
Surely He shall deliver you from the snare of the fowler and from the perilous pestilence.

30. **You Save Me In Troubled Times**
Psalm 138:7
Though I walk in the midst of trouble, You will revive me; You will stretch out Your hand against the wrath of my enemies, and Your right hand will save me.

Nahum 1:7
The Lord is good, a stronghold in the day of trouble; and He knows those who trust in Him.

31. **I Escape Safely**
Psalm 141:10
Let the wicked fall into their own nets, while I escape safely.

32. **You Deliver Me From My Persecutors**
Psalm 142:6
Attend to my cry, for I am brought very low; deliver me from my persecutors, for they are stronger than I.

Psalm 143:9
Deliver me, O Lord, from my enemies; in You I take shelter.

33. **You Deliver Me From Lying Tongues**
Psalm 144:7,11
Stretch out Your hand from above; rescue me and deliver

me out of great waters, from the hand of foreigners. 11 Rescue me and deliver me from the hand of foreigners, whose mouth speaks lying words, and whose right hand is a right hand of falsehood.

34. **He Saves And Preserves Me**
Psalm 145:18-20
The Lord is near to all who call upon Him, to all who call upon Him in truth. 19 He will fulfill the desire of those who fear Him; He also will hear their cry and save them. 20 The Lord preserves all who love Him, but all the wicked He will destroy.

35. **The Lord Is My Deliverer**
2 Samuel 22:2
And he said: "The Lord is my rock and my fortress and my deliverer".

36. **He Will Deliver Me, As He Delivered Daniel**
Daniel 3:17
 If that is the case, our God whom we serve is able to deliver us from the burning fiery furnace, and He will deliver us from your hand, O king.

37. **God Sends His Angels To Deliver Me, As He Did For Daniel, Because I Am Righteous**
Daniel 6:20-22, 27
And when he came to the den, he cried out with a lamenting voice to Daniel. The king spoke, saying to Daniel, "Daniel, servant of the living God, has your God, whom you serve continually, been able to deliver you from the lions?" 21 Then Daniel said to the king, "O king, live forever! 22 My God sent His angel and shut the lions' mouths, so that they have not hurt me, because I was found innocent before Him; and also, O king, I have done no wrong before you." 27 He delivers and rescues, and

He works signs and wonders in heaven and on earth, who has delivered Daniel from the power of the lions.

Proverbs 11:8
The righteous is delivered from trouble, and it comes to the wicked instead.

Psalm 35:17
Lord, how long will You look on? Rescue me from their destructions, my precious life from the lions.

38. **He Delivers Me Because He Delights In Me**
Proverbs 11:19
He also brought me out into a broad place; He delivered me because He delighted in me.

39. **My Seed (Children) Shall Be Delivered**
Proverbs 11:21 (ASV)
Though hand join in hand, the evil man shall not be unpunished; but the seed of the righteous shall be delivered.

Proverbs 11:21
Though they join forces, the wicked will not go unpunished; but the posterity of the righteous will be delivered.

Proverbs 11:21 (TLB)
 You can be very sure the evil man will not go unpunished forever. And you can also be very sure God will rescue the children of the godly.

40. **He Delivers Me, As I Walk Wisely**
Proverbs 28:26
He who trusts in his own heart is a fool, but whoever walks wisely will be delivered.

41. **He Is My Redeemer, Who Calls Me By Name**
Isaiah 43:1
But now, thus says the Lord, who created you, O Jacob, And He who formed you, O Israel: "Fear not, for I have redeemed you; I have called you by your name; You are Mine.

42. **It Is God Who Redeems Me**
Isaiah 44:22
 I have blotted out, like a thick cloud, your transgressions, and like a cloud, your sins. Return to Me, for I have redeemed you.

Isaiah 54:5
For your Maker is your husband, The Lord of hosts is His name; and your Redeemer is the Holy One of Israel; He is called the God of the whole earth.

43. **Fasting Helps In The Deliverance Process**
Isaiah 58:6
Is this not the fast that I have chosen: to loose the bonds of wickedness, to undo the heavy burdens, to let the oppressed go free, and that you break every yoke?

44. **God Is With Me To Save And Deliver Me**
 Jeremiah 15:20-21
And I will make you to this people a fortified bronze wall; and they will fight against you, but they shall not prevail against you; for I am with you to save you and deliver you," says the Lord. 21 "I will deliver you from the hand of the wicked, and I will redeem you from the grip of the terrible."

45. **The Lord Delivers All Who Call On His Name**
Joel 2:32
And it shall come to pass that whoever calls on the name

Deliverance

of the Lord Shall be saved. For in Mount Zion and in Jerusalem there shall be deliverance, as the Lord has said, among the remnant whom the Lord calls.

46. **The Lord Delivers Us From The Evil One**
Matthew 6:13
And do not lead us into temptation, but deliver us from the evil one. For Yours is the kingdom and the power and the glory forever. Amen.

47. **He Delivers The Demon Possessed**
Matthew 8:16
When evening had come, they brought to Him many who were demon-possessed. And He cast out the spirits with a word, and healed all who were sick.

Mark 1:32
At evening, when the sun had set, they brought to Him all who were sick and those who were demon-possessed.

48. **Jesus Delivered Two Demon Possessed Men**
Matthew 8:28-33
When He had come to the other side, to the country of the Gergesenes, there met Him two demon-possessed men, coming out of the tombs, exceedingly fierce, so that no one could pass that way. 29 And suddenly they cried out, saying, "What have we to do with You, Jesus, You Son of God? Have You come here to torment us before the time?" 30 Now a good way off from them there was a herd of many swine feeding. 31 So the demons begged Him, saying, "If You cast us out, permit us to go away into the herd of swine." 32 And He said to them, "Go." So when they had come out, they went into the herd of swine. And suddenly the whole herd of swine ran violently down the steep place into the sea, and perished in the water. 33 Then those who kept them fled; and they

went away into the city and told everything, including what had happened to the demon-possessed men.

49. **Jesus Gave Me Power To Cast Out Demons**
Matthew 10:1
And when He had called His twelve disciples to Him, He gave them power over unclean spirits, to cast them out, and to heal all kinds of sickness and all kinds of disease.

Mark 6:7
And He called the twelve to Himself, and began to send them out two by two, and gave them power over unclean spirits.

Luke 9:1
Then He called His twelve disciples together and gave them power and authority over all demons, and to cure diseases.

50. **Jesus Cast Out Demons By The Spirit Of God**
Matthew 12:22-30
Then one was brought to Him who was demon-possessed, blind and mute; and He healed him, so that the blind and mute man both spoke and saw. 23 And all the multitudes were amazed and said, "Could this be the Son of David?" 24 Now when the Pharisees heard it they said, "This fellow does not cast out demons except by Beelzebub, the ruler of the demons." 25 But Jesus knew their thoughts, and said to them: "Every kingdom divided against itself is brought to desolation, and every city or house divided against itself will not stand. 26 If Satan casts out Satan, he is divided against himself. How then will his kingdom stand? 27 And if I cast out demons by Beelzebub, by whom do your sons cast them out? Therefore they shall be your judges. 28 But if I cast out demons by the Spirit of God, surely the kingdom of God

has come upon you. 29 Or how can one enter a strong man's house and plunder his goods, unless he first binds the strong man? And then he will plunder his house. 30 He who is not with Me is against Me, and he who does not gather with Me scatters abroad".

51. **No Man Is Too Possessed That He Can't Be Delivered**
Mark 5:3-4
Who had *his* dwelling among the tombs; and no one could bind him, not even with chains; 4 because he had often been bound with shackles and chains. And the chains had been pulled apart by him, and the shackles broken in pieces; neither could anyone tame him.

Luke 8:29
For He had commanded the unclean spirit to come out of the man. For it had often seized him, and he was kept under guard, bound with chains and shackles; and he broke the bonds and was driven by the demon into the wilderness.

Mark 5:8-15
For He said to him, "Come out of the man, unclean spirit!" 9 Then He asked him, "What is your name?" And he answered, saying, "My name is Legion; for we are many." 10 Also he begged Him earnestly that He would not send them out of the country. 11 Now a large herd of swine was feeding there near the mountains. 12 So all the demons begged Him, saying, "Send us to the swine, that we may enter them." 13 And at once Jesus gave them permission. Then the unclean spirits went out and entered the swine (there were about two thousand); and the herd ran violently down the steep place into the sea, and drowned in the sea. 14 So those who fed the swine fled, and they told it in the city and in the country. And

they went out to see what it was that had happened. 15 Then they came to Jesus, and saw the one who had been demon-possessed and had the legion, sitting and clothed and in his right mind. And they were afraid.

52. **Demons Are Subject To The Name Of Jesus**
Luke 10:1,17
After these things the Lord appointed seventy others also, and sent them two by two before His face into every city and place where He Himself was about to go. 17 Then the seventy returned with joy, saying, "Lord, even the demons are subject to us in Your name."

53. **God's Word And His Truth Deliver Me And Set Me Free**
John 8:32,36
"And you shall know the truth, and the truth shall make you free." 36 Therefore if the Son makes you free, you shall be free indeed.

54. **God Delivers Supernaturally**
Acts 12:6-7
And when Herod was about to bring him out, that night Peter was sleeping, bound with two chains between two soldiers; and the guards before the door were keeping the prison. 7 Now behold, an angel of the Lord stood by him, and a light shone in the prison; and he struck Peter on the side and raised him up, saying, "Arise quickly!" And his chains fell off his hands.

Acts 16:26
Suddenly there was a great earthquake, so that the foundations of the prison were shaken; and immediately all the doors were opened and everyone's chains were loosed.

55. I Am Free From The Law Of Sin And Death
Romans 8:2
For the law of the Spirit of life in Christ Jesus has made me free from the law of sin and death.

Galatians 5:1
Stand fast therefore in the liberty by which Christ has made us free, and do not be entangled again with a yoke of bondage.

56. I Am Dead To Sin And Alive To God
Romans 6:11-14,18
Likewise you also, reckon yourselves to be dead indeed to sin, but alive to God in Christ Jesus our Lord. 12 Therefore do not let sin reign in your mortal body, that you should obey it in its lusts. 13 And do not present your members as instruments of unrighteousness to sin, but present yourselves to God as being alive from the dead, and your members as instruments of righteousness to God. 14 For sin shall not have dominion over you, for you are not under law but under grace. 18 And having been set free from sin, you became slaves of righteousness.

57. I Am Delivered From The Spirit Of Bondage
Romans 8:15
For you did not receive the spirit of bondage again to fear, but you received the Spirit of adoption by whom we cry out, "Abba, Father."

Hebrews 2:14-15
Inasmuch then as the children have partaken of flesh and blood, He Himself likewise shared in the same, that through death He might destroy him who had the power of death, that is, the devil, 15 and release those who through fear of death were all their lifetime subject to bondage.

58. I Am Delivered From The Evils Of This Present Age
Galatians 1:3-4
Grace to you and peace from God the Father and our Lord Jesus Christ, 4 who gave Himself for our sins, that He might deliver us from this present evil age, according to the will of our God and Father.

59. He Has Delivered Me, And Will Deliver Me
2 Corinthians 1:10
Who delivered us from so great a death, and does deliver us; in whom we trust that He will still deliver us.

Colossians 1:13-14
He has delivered us from the power of darkness and conveyed us into the kingdom of the Son of His love, 14 in whom we have redemption through His blood, the forgiveness of sins.

60. I Am Delivered From The Lust Of My Flesh
1 Corinthians 6:12-13
All things are lawful for me, but all things are not helpful. All things are lawful for me, but I will not be brought under the power of any. 13 Foods for the stomach and the stomach for foods, but God will destroy both it and them. Now the body is not for sexual immorality but for the Lord, and the Lord for the body.

Galatians 5:16-18, 25
I say then: Walk in the Spirit, and you shall not fulfill the lust of the flesh. 17 For the flesh lusts against the Spirit, and the Spirit against the flesh; and these are contrary to one another, so that you do not do the things that you wish. 18 But if you are led by the Spirit, you are not under the law. 25 If we live in the Spirit, let us also walk in the Spirit.

61. As God Delivered Noah, He Will Deliver Me
Hebrews 11:7
By faith Noah, being divinely warned of things not yet seen, moved with godly fear, prepared an ark for the saving of his household, by which he condemned the world and became heir of the righteousness which is according to faith.

62. God Knows How To Deliver Us
2 Peter 2:9-10
Then the Lord knows how to deliver the godly out of temptations and to reserve the unjust under punishment for the day of judgment, 10 and especially those who walk according to the flesh in the lust of uncleanness and despise authority.

63. We May Suffer Persecution, But God Will Deliver Us
2 Timothy 3:10-12
But you have carefully followed my doctrine, manner of life, purpose, faith, longsuffering, love, perseverance, 11 persecutions, afflictions, which happened to me at Antioch, at Iconium, at Lystra--what persecutions I endured. And out of them all the Lord delivered me. 12 Yes, and all who desire to live godly in Christ Jesus will suffer persecution.

64. The Lord Delivers Me From Every Evil Work
2 Timothy 4:18
And the Lord will deliver me from every evil work and preserve me for His heavenly kingdom. To Him be glory forever and ever. Amen!

65. Those Under The Snare Of The Devil Can Be Delivered
2 Timothy 2:25,26

If God perhaps will grant them repentance, so that they may know the truth, 26 and that they may come to their senses and escape the snare of the devil, having been taken captive by him to do his will.

CHAPTER NINE

Favor, Mercy, And Grace

Psalm 5:12
For You, O Lord, will bless the righteous; with favor You will surround him as with a shield.

The favor of God lasts a lifetime. Favor is mostly an Old Testament word. It is found only 8 times in the New Testament. However, God still gives us favor, but the New Testament word used the most is 'grace'. It means unmerited favor.

Like a loving earthly Father, our God is also a compassionate, merciful God. However, there can be no comparison to His eternal mercies or grace! His mercy is everlasting, and new every morning. Lovingkindness is the Old Testament word, which we know as mercy in the New Testament. His favor lasts for a lifetime, and his grace is sufficient.

As you read the scriptures on the favor, mercy and grace of God, answer the following questions.

1. What is the favor of God?
2. What is the mercy of God?
3. What is the grace of God?
4. Who does He give His mercy and grace to?
5. How long does His mercy last?

CHAPTER NINE

Favor

1. **Like My Father Abraham, I Have Found Favor.**
Genesis 18:3
And said, "My Lord, if I have now found favor in Your sight, do not pass on by Your servant".

2. **As Jacob Had Favor That Was Visible, So Do I**
Genesis 30:27
And Laban said to him, "Please stay, if I have found favor in your eyes, for I have learned by experience that the Lord has blessed me for your sake."

3. **Just Like Joseph, I Find Favor And Promotion**
Genesis 39:4
And Joseph found favor in his sight, and he served him; and he made him overseer over his house.

Genesis 39:21
But the Lord was with Joseph and showed him mercy and gave him favor in the sight of the keeper of the prison.

Psalm 75:6,7
For promotion comes neither from the east, nor from the west, nor from the south. 7 But God is the judge; He puts down one, and sets up another.

4. **God Has Given Me Such Favor That All That My Enemies Have Stolen From Me Is Restored**
Exodus 3:21
And I will give this people favor in the sight of the Egyptians; and it shall be, when you go, that you shall not

go empty-handed.

5. God Grants Me Favor In The Midst Of My Enemies
Exodus 11:3
And the Lord gave the people favor in the sight of the Egyptians. Moreover the man Moses was very great in the land of Egypt, in the sight of Pharaoh's servants and in the sight of the people.

Exodus 12:36
And the Lord had given the people favor in the sight of the Egyptians, so that they granted them what they requested. Thus they plundered the Egyptians.

Psalm 41:11
By this I know that You favor and delight in me, because my enemy does not triumph over me.

6. God Grants Me Favor In Real Estate And Land
Deuteronomy 33:23
And of Naphtali he said: "O Naphtali, satisfied with favor, And full of the blessing of the Lord, Possess the west and the south."

Psalm 44:3
For they did not gain possession of the land by their own sword, nor did their own arm save them; but it was Your right hand, Your arm, and the light of Your countenance, because You favored them.

Deuteronomy 6:11
Houses full of all good things, which you did not fill, hewn-out wells which you did not dig, vineyards and olive trees which you did not plant—when you have eaten and are full.

7. God Gives Me Favor Even Though I Seem The Least Likely To Receive It
1 Samuel 16:22
Then Saul sent to Jesse, saying, "Please let David stand before me, for he has found favor in my sight."

8. God Gives Me Great Favor In All My Battles
Joshua 11:20
For it was of the Lord to harden their hearts that they should come against Israel in battle that he might destroy them utterly and that they may have no favor, but that he might destroy them as the Lord commanded Moses.

9. God Is Looking For Me To Show Me His Favor
2 Chronicles 16:9
For the eyes of the Lord run to and fro throughout the whole earth, to show Himself strong on behalf of those whose heart is loyal to Him.

10. Like Ruth, I Have Favor In Other Countries
Ruth 2:10-13
So she fell on her face, bowed down to the ground, and said to him, "Why have I found favor in your eyes, that you should take notice of me, since I am a foreigner?" 13 Then she said, "Let me find favor in your sight, my lord; for you have comforted me, and have spoken kindly to your maidservant, though I am not like one of your maidservants."

11. Like Hannah, I Have Favor With My Prayers, And My Offspring Is Favored
1 Samuel 1:18
And she said, "Let your maidservant find favor in your sight." So the woman went her way and ate, and her face was no longer sad.

1 Samuel 2:26
And the child Samuel grew in stature, and in favor both with the Lord and men.

12. **Like Esther, I Am Highly Favored Among All Others With Special Treatment And Recognition**
Esther 2:9, 15,17
Now the young woman pleased him, and she obtained his favor; so he readily gave beauty preparations to her, besides her allowance. Then seven choice maidservants were provided for her from the king's palace, and he moved her and her maidservants to the best place in the house of the women. 15 Now when the turn came for Esther the daughter of Abihail the uncle of Mordecai, who had taken her as his daughter, to go in to the king, she requested nothing but what Hegai the king's eunuch, the custodian of the women, advised. And Esther obtained favor in the sight of all who saw her. 17 The king loved Esther more than all the other women, and she obtained grace and favor in his sight more than all the virgins; so he set the royal crown upon her head and made her queen instead of Vashti.

13. **God's Favor Grants Petitions By Even Ungodly Civil Authority**
Esther 5:2,8
So it was, when the king saw Queen Esther standing in the court, that she found favor in his sight, and the king held out to Esther the golden scepter that was in his hand. Then Esther went near and touched the top of the scepter. 8 "If I have found favor in the sight of the king, and if it pleases the king to grant my petition and fulfill my request, then let the king and Haman come to the banquet which I will prepare for them, and tomorrow I will do as the king has said."

14. God's Favor Changes Government Regulations, If Need Be, For Me
Esther 7:3
Then Queen Esther answered and said, "If I have found favor in your sight, O king, and if it pleases the king, let my life be given me at my petition, and my people at my request".

Esther 8:5
And said, "If it pleases the king, and if I have found favor in his sight and the thing seems right to the king and I am pleasing in his eyes, let it be written to revoke the letters devised by Haman, the son of Hammedatha the Agagite, which he wrote to annihilate the Jews who are in all the king's provinces".

16. God Surrounds Me With Favor, Like A Shield
Psalm 5:12
For You, O Lord, will bless the righteous; with favor You will surround him as with a shield.

17. God's Favor On Me Is For A Lifetime
Psalm 30:5
For His anger is but for a moment, but His favor is for a lifetime, or in His favor is life.

18. God Favors My Works
Psalm 35:27
Let them shout for joy and be glad, who favor my righteous cause; and let them say continually, "Let the Lord be magnified, who has pleasure in the prosperity of His servant."

Psalm 90:17
And let the beauty and delightfulness and favor of the

Lord our God be upon us; confirm and establish the work of our hands-yes, the work of our hands, confirm and establish it.

19. **You Favor Me With Goodness, Abundance And Ease**
Psalm 65:11
You crown the year with Your goodness, and Your paths drip with abundance.

Job 29:6
When my steps were bathed with cream, and the rock poured out rivers of oil for me!

20. **God Gives Me Favor And Withholds Nothing From Me**
Psalm 84:11
For the Lord God is a sun and shield; the Lord bestows favor and honor; no good thing does he withhold from those whose walk is blameless.

Job 10:12
You have granted me life and favor, and Your care has preserved my spirit.

21. **You, God, Give Me Favor And Perfect Everything That Concerns Me Because Of Your Mercy**
Psalm 119:58
I entreated Your favor with my whole heart; be merciful to me according to Your word.

Psalm 138:8
The Lord will perfect that which concerns me; Your mercy, O Lord, endures forever; do not forsake the works of Your hands.

22. **God Grants Favor To Me As I Walk In Truth**
Proverbs 3:4
Let not mercy and truth forsake you; bind them around your neck, write them on the tablet of your heart, and so find favor and high esteem In the sight of God and man.

Proverbs 8:35
For whoever finds me finds life, and obtains favor from the Lord.

Proverbs 11:27
He who earnestly seeks good finds favor, but trouble will come to him who seeks evil.

Proverbs 12:2
A good man obtains favor from the Lord, but a man of wicked intentions He will condemn.

Proverbs 13:15
Good understanding gains favor, but the way of the unfaithful is hard.

Proverbs 14:9
Fools mock at sin, but among the upright there is favor.

23. **Whoever Finds A Wife Finds Favor From The Lord**
Proverbs 18:22
He who finds a wife finds a good thing, and obtains favor from the Lord.

24. **The Kings Favor Is Refreshing**
Proverbs 19:12
The king's wrath is like the roaring of a lion, but his favor is like dew on the grass.

25. A Good Name Brings Favor
Proverbs 22:1
A good name is to be chosen rather than great riches, loving favor rather than silver and gold.

26. Whoever Corrects A Man Will Find Favor
Proverbs 28:23
He who rebukes a man will find more favor afterward than he who flatters with the tongue.

27. Like Mary, I Am Highly Favored By God
Luke 1:28
And having come in, the angel said to her, "Rejoice, highly favored one, the Lord is with you; blessed are you among women!"

Luke 1:30
Then the angel said to her, "Do not be afraid, Mary, for you have found favor with God".

28. I Have Favor With God And Man
Luke 2:52
And Jesus increased in wisdom and stature, and in favor with God and men.

Acts 2:47
…praising God and having favor with all the people. And the Lord added to the church daily those who were being saved.

29. I Have Favor As I Am Diligent
Proverbs 10:4
He who has a slack hand becomes poor, but the hand of the diligent makes rich.

Psalm 112:5
It is well with the man who deals generously and lends, who conducts his affairs with justice.

30. **As I Please God, He Gives Me Favor With My Enemies**
Proverbs 16:7
When a man's ways please the Lord, He makes even his enemies to be at peace with him.

31. **God Favors The Saints**
Luke 2:14
Glory to God in the highest and on earth peace to men on whom His favor rests.

Daniel 7:22
Until the Ancient of Days came, and a judgment was made in favor of the saints of the Most High, and the time came for the saints to possess the kingdom.

32. **Like Men Of God Before Me, I Have The Favor Of God**
Acts 7:10
And delivered him out of all his troubles, and gave him favor and wisdom in the presence of Pharaoh, king of Egypt; and he made him governor over Egypt and all his house.

Acts 7:46
Who found favor before God and asked to find a dwelling for the God of Jacob.

Daniel 1:9
Now God had brought Daniel into the favor and goodwill of the chief of the eunuchs.

33. Today Is My Day Of Favor
2 Corinthians 6:2 (NIV)
For He says "In the time of my favor I heard you, and in the day of salvation I helped you". I tell you, now is the time of God's favor, now is the day of salvation.

Mercy

34. God's Mercy Endures Forever
1 Chronicles 16:34
Oh, give thanks to the Lord for He is good! For His mercy endures forever.

2 Chronicles 5:13
And praised the Lord, saying: "For He is good, For His mercy endures forever," that the house, the house of the Lord, was filled with a cloud.

2 Chronicles 7:3
When all the children of Israel saw how the fire came down, and the glory of the Lord on the temple, they bowed their faces to the ground on the pavement, and worshiped and praised the Lord, saying: "For He is good, For His mercy endures forever."

35. God Is Gracious And Merciful
Nehemiah 9:31-32
Nevertheless in Your great mercy You did not utterly consume them nor forsake them; for You are God, gracious and merciful. 32 "Now therefore, our God, the great, the mighty, and awesome God, who keeps covenant and mercy".

Deuteronomy 5:10
But showing mercy to thousands, to those who love Me and keep My commandments.

36. **God Is Merciful To The Merciful**
2 Samuel 22:26-27
With the merciful You will show Yourself merciful; with a blameless man You will show Yourself blameless; 27 with the pure You will show Yourself pure; and with the devious You will show Yourself shrewd.

37. **God's Mercies Are Greater Than Man's**
2 Samuel 24:14
And David said to Gad, "I am in great distress. Please let us fall into the hand of the Lord, for His mercies are great; but do not let me fall into the hand of man."

38. **His Mercy Follows Me**
Psalm 23:6
Surely goodness and mercy shall follow me all the days of my life; and I will dwell in the house of the Lord Forever.

39. **God's Is A God Of Mercy And Truth**
Psalm 25:10
All the paths of the Lord are mercy and truth, to such as keep His covenant and His testimonies.

Psalm 57:10
For Your mercy reaches unto the heavens, and Your truth unto the clouds.

Psalm 85:10
Mercy and truth have met together; righteousness and peace have kissed.

Psalm 86:15
But You, O Lord, are a God full of compassion, and gracious, longsuffering and abundant in mercy and truth.

Psalm 89:14
Righteousness and justice are the foundation of Your throne; mercy and truth go before Your face.

Psalm 100:5
For the Lord is good; His mercy is everlasting, and His truth endures to all generations.

Psalm 108:4
For Your mercy is great above the heavens, and Your truth reaches to the clouds.

Psalm 89:14
Righteousness and justice are the foundation of Your throne; mercy and truth go before Your face.

Psalm 115:1
Not unto us, O Lord, not unto us, but to Your name give glory, because of Your mercy, because of Your truth.

Proverbs 20:28
Mercy and truth preserve the king, and by lovingkindness he upholds his throne.

40. God Is Merciful Towards Sinners
Psalm 25:7
Do not remember the sins of my youth, nor my transgressions; According to Your mercy remember me, For Your goodness' sake, O Lord.

Matthew 9:13
But go and learn what this means: 'I desire mercy and not sacrifice.' For I did not come to call the righteous, but sinners, to repentance."

Luke 18:13
And the tax collector, standing afar off, would not so much as raise his eyes to heaven, but beat his breast, saying, 'God, be merciful to me a sinner!'

Romans 11:30-32
For as you were once disobedient to God, yet have now obtained mercy through their disobedience, 31 even so these also have now been disobedient, that through the mercy shown you they also may obtain mercy. 32 For God has committed them all to disobedience, that He might have mercy on all.

Hebrews 8:12
 For I will be merciful to their unrighteousness, and their sins and their lawless deeds I will remember no more.

1 Peter 2:10
Who once were not a people but are now the people of God, who had not obtained mercy but now have obtained mercy.

41. **The Lord Is Slow To Anger And Abounds In Mercy**
 Psalm 103:8
The Lord is merciful and gracious, slow to anger, and abounding in mercy.

Psalm 103:11
For as the heavens are high above the earth, so great is His mercy toward those who fear Him.

Jonah 4:2
So he prayed to the Lord, and said, "Ah, Lord, was not this what I said when I was still in my country? Therefore I fled previously to Tarshish; for I know that You are a gracious and merciful God, slow to anger and abundant in lovingkindness, one who relents from doing harm".

Psalm 86:5
For You, Lord, are good, and ready to forgive, and abundant in mercy to all those who call upon You.

Ephesians 2:4
But God, who is rich in mercy, because of His great love with which He loved us.

42. **God's Mercy Is Everlasting To Those Who Fear Him**
Psalm 100:5
For the Lord is good; His mercy is everlasting, and His truth endures to all generations.

Psalm 103:17
But the mercy of the Lord is from everlasting to everlasting on those who fear Him, and His righteousness to children's children.

Daniel 9:4
And I prayed to the Lord my God, and made confession, and said, "O Lord, great and awesome God, who keeps His covenant and mercy with those who love Him, and with those who keep His commandments".

1 Kings 8:23
...and he said: "Lord God of Israel, there is no God in heaven above or on earth below like You, who keep Your covenant and mercy with Your servants who walk before

You with all their hearts".

43. **God Crowns Me With Lovingkindness And Mercy**
Psalm 63:3
Because Your lovingkindness is better than life, my lips shall praise You.

Hosea 2:19
I will betroth you to Me forever; Yes, I will betroth you to Me In righteousness and justice, in lovingkindness and mercy.

Psalm 103:2-4
Bless the Lord, O my soul, and forget not all His benefits: 3 who forgives all your iniquities, who heals all your diseases, 4 who redeems your life from destruction, who crowns you with lovingkindness and tender mercies.

44. **His Mercies Are New Every Morning**
Lamentations 3:22-23
Through the Lord's mercies we are not consumed, because His compassions fail not. 23 They are new every morning; great is Your faithfulness.

45. **God Loves Mercy**
Micah 6:8
He has shown you, O man, what is good; and what does the Lord require of you but to do justly, to love mercy, and to walk humbly with your God?

Micah 7:18
Who is a God like You, pardoning iniquity and passing over the transgression of the remnant of His heritage? He does not retain His anger forever, because He delights in mercy.

46. God Wants Me To Be Merciful, As He Is
Luke 6:36
Therefore be merciful, just as your Father also is merciful.

Luke 10:37
And he said, "He who showed mercy on him." Then Jesus said to him, "Go and do likewise."

Jude 1:2
Mercy, peace, and love be multiplied to you.

Jude 1:21
…keep yourselves in the love of God, looking for the mercy of our Lord Jesus Christ unto eternal life.

Zechariah 7:9
Thus says the Lord of hosts: 'Execute true justice, show mercy and compassion everyone to his brother'.

47. God Has Mercy On Whom He Wills
Romans 9:15-16
For He says to Moses, "I will have mercy on whomever I will have mercy, and I will have compassion on whomever I will have compassion." So then it is not of him who wills, nor of him who runs, but of God who shows mercy.

Romans 9:18
Therefore He has mercy on whom He wills, and whom He wills He hardens.

48. Mercy Triumphs Over Judgment
James 2:13
For judgment is without mercy to the one who has shown no mercy. Mercy triumphs over judgment.

49. I Have Now Obtained Mercy
1 Peter 2:9-10
But you are a chosen generation, a royal priesthood, a holy nation, His own special people, that you may proclaim the praises of Him who called you out of darkness into His marvelous light; 10 who once were not a people but are now the people of God, who had not obtained mercy but now have obtained mercy.

Grace

50. God Grants Me Grace In The Midst Of A Perverse Generation
Genesis 6:7-8
So the Lord said, "I will destroy man whom I have created from the face of the earth, both man and beast, creeping thing and birds of the air, for I am sorry that I have made them." 8 But Noah found grace in the eyes of the Lord.

51. God Is Good, Gracious And Compassionate To Me
Exodus 33:13
"Now therefore, I pray, if I have found grace in Your sight, show me now Your way, that I may know You and that I may find grace in Your sight. And consider that this nation is Your people."

Exodus 33:17-19
So the Lord said to Moses, "I will also do this thing that you have spoken; for you have found grace in My sight, and I know you by name." 18 And he said, "Please, show me Your glory." 19 Then He said, "I will make all My goodness pass before you, and I will proclaim the name

of the Lord before you. I will be gracious to whom I will be gracious, and I will have compassion on whom I will have compassion."

Exodus 34:9
Then he said, "If now I have found grace in Your sight, O Lord, let my Lord, I pray, go among us, even though we are a stiff-necked people; and pardon our iniquity and our sin, and take us as Your inheritance."

Psalm 27:13
I would have lost heart, unless I had believed that I would see the goodness of the Lord In the land of the living.

Psalm 107:8-9
Oh that men would give thanks to the Lord for His goodness, and for His wonderful works to the children of men! 9 For He satisfies the longing soul, and fills the hungry soul with goodness.

Psalm 31:19
Oh, how great is Your goodness, which You have laid up for those who fear You, which You have prepared for those who trust in You in the presence of the sons of men!

Psalm 111:4
He has made His wonderful works to be remembered; the Lord is gracious and full of compassion.

52. God's Word (Wisdom) Is Like A Graceful Ornament To Me
Proverbs 1:9
For they will be a graceful ornament on your head, and chains about your neck.

Proverbs 3:22
So they will be life to your soul and grace to your neck.

Proverbs 4:9
She will place on your head an ornament of grace; a crown of glory she will deliver to you.

53. I Speak Grace To The Mountains In My Life
Zechariah 4:6-7
So he answered and said to me: "This is the word of the Lord to Zerubbabel: 'Not by might nor by power, but by My Spirit,' Says the LORD of hosts. 7 'Who are you, O great mountain? Before Zerubbabel you shall become a plain! And he shall bring forth the capstone with shouts of "Grace, grace to it!" ' "

54. God Resists The Proud But Gives Grace To The Humble
James 4:6
But He gives more grace. Therefore He says: "God resists the proud, But gives grace to the humble."

1 Peter 5:5
Likewise you younger people, submit yourselves to your elders. Yes, all of you be submissive to one another, and be clothed with humility, for "God resists the proud, but gives grace to the humble."

Proverbs 3:34
Surely He scorns the scornful, but gives grace to the humble.

55. I Have Received Grace And Truth Through Jesus
John 1:14,16-17
And the Word became flesh and dwelt among us, and we

beheld His glory, the glory as of the only begotten of the Father, full of grace and truth. 16 And of His fullness we have all received, and grace for grace. 17 For the law was given through Moses, but grace and truth came through Jesus Christ.

Colossians 1:5-6
Because of the hope which is laid up for you in heaven, of which you heard before in the word of the truth of the gospel, 6 which has come to you, as it has also in all the world, and is bringing forth fruit, as it is also among you since the day you heard and knew the grace of God in truth.

2 John 1:3
Grace, mercy, and peace will be with you from God the Father and from the Lord Jesus Christ, the Son of the Father, in truth and love.

56. **God's Grace Is Upon Me**
Acts 4:33
And with great power the apostles gave witness to the resurrection of the Lord Jesus. And great grace was upon them all.

Luke 2:40
And the Child grew and became strong in spirit, filled with wisdom; and the grace of God was upon Him.

Acts 20:24
But none of these things move me; nor do I count my life dear to myself, so that I may finish my race with joy, and the ministry which I received from the Lord Jesus, to testify to the gospel of the grace of God.

57. **Through God's Grace I Reign In Life**
Romans 5:15,17
But the free gift is not like the offense. For if by the one man's offense many died, much more the grace of God and the gift by the grace of the one Man, Jesus Christ, abounded to many. 17 For if by the one man's offense death reigned through the one, much more those who receive abundance of grace and of the gift of righteousness will reign in life through the One, Jesus Christ.

58. **Where Sin Abounds, Grace Abounds More**
Romans 5:20-21
Moreover the law entered that the offense might abound. But where sin abounded, grace abounded much more. 21 So that as sin reigned in death, even so grace might reign through righteousness to eternal life through Jesus Christ our Lord.

59. **I Am Not Under The Law, But Under Grace**
Romans 6:1,14,15
What shall we say then? Shall we continue in sin that grace may abound? For sin shall not have dominion over you, for you are not under law but under grace. 15 What then? Shall we sin because we are not under law but under grace? Certainly not!

60. **I Am What I Am By The Grace Of God; I Speak By His Grace**
1 Corinthians 15:10
But by the grace of God I am what I am, and His grace toward me was not in vain; but I labored more abundantly than they all, yet not I, but the grace of God which was with me.

Colossians 4:6
Let your speech always be with grace, seasoned with salt, that you may know how you ought to answer each one.

61. **Because Of The Grace Of God, I Am Made Rich And Amply Supplied**
2 Corinthians 8:9
For you know the grace of our Lord Jesus Christ, that though He was rich, yet for your sakes He became poor, that you through His poverty might become rich.

2 Corinthians 9:8
And God is able to make all grace abound toward you, that you, always having all sufficiency in all things, may have an abundance for every good work.

Psalm 84:11
For the Lord God is a sun and shield; the Lord will give grace and glory; no good thing will He withhold from those who walk uprightly.

62. **God's Grace Is Sufficient For Me**
2 Corinthians 12:9
and He said to me, "My grace is sufficient for you, for My strength is made perfect in weakness." Therefore most gladly I will rather boast in my infirmities, that the power of Christ may rest upon me.

Acts 20:32
So now, brethren, I commend you to God and to the word of His grace, which is able to build you up and give you an inheritance among all those who are sanctified.

63. **I Am Saved And I Serve By His Gift Of Grace**
Ephesians 2:8

For by grace you have been saved through faith, and that not of yourselves; it is the gift of God.

Hebrews 12:28
Therefore, since we are receiving a kingdom which cannot be shaken, let us have grace, by which we may serve God acceptably with reverence and godly fear.

64. **I Come Boldly To His Throne Of Grace**
Hebrews 4:16
Let us therefore come boldly to the throne of grace, that we may obtain mercy and find grace to help in time of need.

65. **I Do Not Insult Or Fall Short Of The Grace Of God**
Hebrews 10:29
Of how much worse punishment, do you suppose, will he be thought worthy who has trampled the Son of God underfoot, counted the blood of the covenant by which he was sanctified a common thing, and insulted the Spirit of grace?

Hebrews 12:15
…looking carefully lest anyone fall short of the grace of God; lest any root of bitterness springing up cause trouble, and by this many become defiled.

Hebrews 12:28
Therefore, since we are receiving a kingdom which cannot be shaken, let us have grace, by which we may serve God acceptably with reverence and godly fear.

Galatians 2:21
I do not set aside the grace of God; for if righteousness comes through the law, then Christ died in vain.

CHAPTER TEN

Restoration And Justice

Luke 18:7
And shall God not avenge His own elect who cry out day and night to Him, though He bears long with them?

The theme of restoration is woven in and out of scripture, from Genesis to Revelation. Why? Because God is a restorer. God is the original avenger! In our day, there is a strong justice movement. This is the very heart beat of God. His heart is broken by all of the terrible injustices of our day. His desire for justice and restoration is getting stronger, as we approach His soon coming return.

God is also judge of all. He is coming to judge the living and the dead. He will bring justice. He will judge the earth. Every man will give account to Him.

As you meditate on the following scriptures about the justice of God, answer these questions.

1. Does God desire to bring restoration?
2. How does God feel when He sees injustice?
3. Is God a vengeful God?
4. Who is the rightful judge of all the earth?
5. How does knowing that God will vindicate His children make you feel about Him?

CHAPTER TEN

Restoration And Justice

1. God Is Judge Of All The Earth
Genesis 18:25
Far be it from You to do such a thing as this, to slay the righteous with the wicked, so that the righteous should be as the wicked; far be it from You! Shall not the Judge of all the earth do right?

Ecclesiastes 3:17
I said in my heart, "God shall judge the righteous and the wicked, for there is a time there for every purpose and for every work."

2. Vindication Belongs To God
Genesis 50:15, 20
When Joseph's brothers saw that their father was dead, they said, "Perhaps Joseph will hate us, and may actually repay us for all the evil which we did to him." 20 But as for you, you meant evil against me; but God meant it for good, in order to bring it about as it is this day, to save many people alive.

3. Restoration Is In The Covenant
Exodus 22:1,4
If a man steals an ox or a sheep, and slaughters it or sells it, he shall restore five oxen for an ox and four sheep for a sheep. 4 If the theft is certainly found alive in his hand, whether it is an ox or donkey or sheep, he shall restore double.

4. Justice And Vengeance Belong To God
Exodus 32:26-28

...then Moses stood in the entrance of the camp, and said, "Whoever is on the Lord's side—come to me!" And all the sons of Levi gathered themselves together to him. 27 And he said to them, "Thus says the Lord God of Israel: 'Let every man put his sword on his side, and go in and out from entrance to entrance throughout the camp, and let every man kill his brother, every man his companion, and every man his neighbor.'" 28 So the sons of Levi did according to the word of Moses. And about three thousand men of the people fell that day.

5. **God's Desire Is For Restoration**
Deuteronomy 30:3
That the Lord your God will bring you back from captivity, and have compassion on you, and gather you again from all the nations where the Lord your God has scattered you.

6. **God Will Render Justice To His Adversaries**
Deuteronomy 32:43
Rejoice, O Gentiles, with His people; for He will avenge the blood of His servants, and render vengeance to His adversaries; He will provide atonement for His land and His people.

7. **The Lord Sees And Repays**
Ruth 2:12
The Lord repay your work, and a full reward be given you by the Lord God of Israel, under whose wings you have come for refuge.

1 Samuel 26:23
May the Lord repay every man for his righteousness and his faithfulness; for the Lord delivered you into my hand today, but I would not stretch out my hand against the Lord's anointed.

2 Samuel 2:6
And now may the Lord show kindness and truth to you. I also will repay you this kindness, because you have done this thing.

8. I Pursue, Overtake, And Recover All
1 Samuel 30:8,18,19
Pursue, overtake and recover all. 18 So David recovered all that the Amalekites had carried away, and David rescued his two wives. 19 And nothing of theirs was lacking, either small or great, sons or daughters, spoil or anything which they had taken from them; David recovered all.

9. God Remembers His Covenant And Restores
2 Samuel 9:7
So David said to him, "Do not fear, for I will surely show you kindness for Jonathan your father's sake, and will restore to you all the land of Saul your grandfather; and you shall eat bread at my table continually."

Job 34:11
For He repays man according to his work, and makes man to find a reward according to his way.

10. The Lord Rewards The Righteous
2 Samuel 22:21
The Lord rewarded me according to my righteousness; according to the cleanness of my hands He has recompensed me.

Psalm 91:8
Only with your eyes shall you look, and see the reward of the wicked.

Proverbs 11:18
The wicked man does deceptive work, but he who sows righteousness will have a sure reward.

Proverbs 13:13
He who despises the word will be destroyed, but he who fears the commandment will be rewarded.

11. **The Lord Is Judge Of The Earth**
1 Chronicles 16:31-33
Let the heavens rejoice, and let the earth be glad; and let them say among the nations, "The Lord reigns." 32 Let the sea roar, and all its fullness; let the field rejoice, and all that is in it. 33 Then the trees of the woods shall rejoice before the Lord, for He is coming to judge the earth.

Psalm 58:10-11
The righteous shall rejoice when he sees the vengeance; he shall wash his feet in the blood of the wicked, 11 So that men will say, "Surely there is a reward for the righteous; surely He is God who judges in the earth."

Psalm 82:8
Arise, O God; judge the earth; for You shall inherit all nations.

12. **God Restores Man To Righteousness**
Job 33:26
He shall pray to God, and He will delight in him, He shall see His face with joy, for He restores to man His righteousness.

13. **Repentance Brings Restoration To God**
Job 33:30

Then he looks at men and says, 'I have sinned, and perverted what was right, and it did not profit me.' To bring back his soul from the Pit, that he may be enlightened with the light of life.

14. God Brings Justice And Does Not Oppress
Job 37:23
As for the Almighty, we cannot find Him; He is excellent in power, in judgment and abundant justice; He does not oppress.

Psalm 10:18
To do justice to the fatherless and the oppressed, that the man of the earth may oppress no more.

15. God Restores Double For Our Loss
Job 42:10,12
And the Lord restored Job's losses when he prayed for his friends. Indeed the Lord gave Job twice as much as he had before. 12 So the Lord blessed the latter end of Job more than the beginning.

Job 42:13-16
He also had seven sons and three daughters. 14 And he called the name of the first Jemimah, the name of the second Keziah, and the name of the third Keren-Happuch. 15 In all the land were found no women so beautiful as the daughters of Job; and their father gave them an inheritance among their brothers. 16 After this Job lived one hundred and forty years, and saw his children and grandchildren for four generations.

16. God Is A Just Judge
Psalm 7:8,11, 14-16
The Lord shall judge the peoples; Judge me, O Lord, according to my righteousness, and according to my

integrity within me. 11 God is a just judge, and God is angry with the wicked every day. 14 Behold, the wicked brings forth iniquity; Yes, he conceives trouble and brings forth falsehood. 15 He made a pit and dug it out, and has fallen into the ditch which he made. 16 His trouble shall return upon his own head, and his violent dealing shall come down on his own crown.

17. **God Judges In Righteousness**
Psalm 9:8
He shall judge the world in righteousness, and He shall administer judgment for the peoples in uprightness.

Psalm 50:4,6
He shall call to the heavens from above, and to the earth, that He may judge His people: 6 Let the heavens declare His righteousness, For God Himself is Judge. Selah

Psalm 72:2
He will judge Your people with righteousness, and Your poor with justice.

Jeremiah 11:20
But, O Lord of hosts, You who judge righteously, testing the mind and the heart, let me see Your vengeance on them, for to You I have revealed my cause.

John 5:30
I can of Myself do nothing. As I hear, I judge; and My judgment is righteous, because I do not seek My own will but the will of the Father who sent Me.

18. **God Vindicates His Children**
Psalm 54:5
He will repay my enemies for their evil. Cut them off in Your truth.

Psalm 26:1
Vindicate me, O Lord, for I have walked in my integrity. I have also trusted in the Lord; I shall not slip.

19. God Is A God Of Justice
Psalm 10:18
To do justice to the fatherless and the oppressed, that the man of the earth may oppress no more.

Proverbs 29:26
Many seek the ruler's favor, but justice for man comes from the Lord.

Job 34:12
Surely God will never do wickedly, nor will the Almighty pervert justice.

20. God Restores My Soul
Psalm 23:3
He restores my soul; He leads me in the paths of righteousness For His name's sake.

Psalm 51:12
Restore to me the joy of Your salvation, and uphold me by Your generous Spirit.

21. God Can Turn Around Any Situation
Psalm 30:5
For His anger is but for a moment, His favor is for life; weeping may endure for a night, but joy comes in the morning.

Isaiah 61:2-3
To proclaim the acceptable year of the Lord, and the day of vengeance of our God; to comfort all who mourn, 3 to

Restoration And Justice

console those who mourn in Zion, to give them beauty for ashes, the oil of joy for mourning, the garment of praise for the spirit of heaviness; that they may be called trees of righteousness, the planting of the Lord, that He may be glorified.

22. **You Vindicate Me And Deliver Me**
Psalm 43:1
Vindicate me, O God, and plead my cause against an ungodly nation; Oh, deliver me from the deceitful and unjust man!

Psalm 35:24
Vindicate me, O Lord my God, according to Your righteousness; and let them not rejoice over me.

23. **God Brings Justice To The Poor**
Psalm 72:4
He will bring justice to the poor of the people; He will save the children of the needy, and will break in pieces the oppressor.

Psalm 82:3-4
Defend the poor and fatherless; do justice to the afflicted and needy. 4 Deliver the poor and needy; free them from the hand of the wicked.

24. **You Restore Us, God**
Psalm 60:1
O God, You have cast us off; You have broken us down; You have been displeased; Oh, restore us again!

Psalm 80:3
Restore us, O God; cause Your face to shine, and we shall be saved!

Psalm 80:7
Restore us, O God of hosts; cause Your face to shine, and we shall be saved!

Psalm 80:19
Restore us, O Lord God of hosts; cause Your face to shine, and we shall be saved!

Psalm 85:4
Restore us, O God of our salvation, and cause Your anger toward us to cease.

Psalm 85:6
Will You not revive us again, that Your people may rejoice in You?

25. **God Is A Defender Of The Widows And Orphans**
Psalm 68:5
A father of the fatherless, a defender of widows, is God in His holy habitation.

Psalm 146:9
The Lord watches over the strangers; He relieves the fatherless and widow; but the way of the wicked He turns upside down.

Jeremiah 7:6-7
if you do not oppress the stranger, the fatherless, and the widow, and do not shed innocent blood in this place, or walk after other gods to your hurt, 7 then I will cause you to dwell in this place, in the land that I gave to your fathers forever and ever.

James 1:27
Pure and undefiled religion before God and the Father is

this: to visit orphans and widows in their trouble, and to keep oneself unspotted from the world.

26. **You Execute Righteousness And Justice**
Psalm 89:14
Righteousness and justice are the foundation of Your throne; mercy and truth go before Your face.

Psalm 97:2
Clouds and darkness surround Him; righteousness and justice are the foundation of His throne.

Psalm 103:6
The Lord executes righteousness and justice for all who are oppressed.

27. **Vengeance Belongs To God**
Psalm 94:1-2
O Lord God, to whom vengeance belongs-- O God, to whom vengeance belongs, shine forth! 2 Rise up, O Judge of the earth; render punishment to the proud.

Psalm 94:16-17
Who will rise up for me against the evildoers? Who will stand up for me against the workers of iniquity? 17 Unless the Lord had been my help, my soul would soon have settled in silence.

28. **The Thief Must Restore Seven Fold**
Proverbs 6:30-31
People do not despise the thief if he steals to satisfy his hunger when he is starving. 31 Yet if he is caught, he must pay sevenfold, though it cost him all the wealth of his house.

29. The Lord Rewards Acts Of Goodness
Proverbs 25:21-22
If your enemy is hungry, give him bread to eat; and if he is thirsty, give him water to drink; 22 For so you will heap coals of fire on his head, and the Lord will reward you.

Romans 12:20-21
Therefore "If your enemy is hungry, feed him; if he is thirsty, give him a drink; for in so doing you will heap coals of fire on his head." 21 Do not be overcome by evil, but overcome evil with good.

30. God Defends The Poor And Needy
Isaiah 1:17
Learn to do good; seek justice, rebuke the oppressor; defend the fatherless, plead for the widow.

Psalm 82:3-4
Defend the poor and fatherless; do justice to the afflicted and needy. 4 Deliver the poor and needy; free them from the hand of the wicked.

31. God Is The Judge Of What Is Good And Evil
Isaiah 5:20
Woe to those who call evil good, and good evil; who put darkness for light, and light for darkness; who put bitter for sweet, and sweet for bitter!

32. We Say Restore
Isaiah 42:22
But this is a people robbed and plundered; all of them are snared in holes, and they are hidden in prison houses; they are for prey, and no one delivers; for plunder, and no one says, "Restore!"

33. **God Is Bringing Our Sons And Daughters Home**
Isaiah 43: 5-6
Fear not, for I am with you; I will bring your descendants from the east, and gather you from the west; 6 I will say to the north, 'Give them up!' And to the south, 'Do not keep them back!' Bring My sons from afar, and My daughters from the ends of the earth.

Isaiah 60:4
Lift up your eyes all around, and see: They all gather together, they come to you; your sons shall come from afar, and your daughters shall be nursed at your side.

34. **God's Plan Is Restoration**
Isaiah 58:12
Those from among you shall build the old waste places; you shall raise up the foundations of many generations; and you shall be called the Repairer of the Breach, The Restorer of Streets to Dwell In.

Isaiah 61:4
And they shall rebuild the old ruins, they shall raise up the former desolations, and they shall repair the ruined cities, the desolations of many generations.

35. **God Restores Double, And Removes Reproach**
Isaiah 25:8 (NIV)
He will swallow up death forever. The Sovereign Lord will wipe away the tears from all faces; He will remove his people's disgrace from all the earth. The Lord has spoken.

Isaiah 54:4
Do not fear, for you will not be ashamed; neither be disgraced, for you will not be put to shame; for you will

forget the shame of your youth, and will not remember the reproach of your widowhood anymore.

Isaiah 61:7
Instead of your shame you will receive a double portion, and instead of disgrace you will rejoice in your inheritance. And so you will inherit a double portion in your land, and everlasting joy will be yours.

Joel 2:18-19
Then the Lord will be zealous for His land, and pity His people.19 The Lord will answer and say to His people, "Behold, I will send you grain and new wine and oil, and you will be satisfied by them; I will no longer make you a reproach among the nations.

36. God Desires To Restore The Backsliders
Jeremiah 3:12-14
Go and proclaim these words toward the north, and say: 'Return, backsliding Israel,' says the Lord; 'I will not cause My anger to fall on you. For I am merciful,' says the Lord; ' I will not remain angry forever. 13 Only acknowledge your iniquity, that you have transgressed against the Lord your God, and have scattered your charms to alien deities under every green tree, and you have not obeyed My voice,' says the Lord. 14 "Return, O backsliding children," says the Lord; "for I am married to you. I will take you, one from a city and two from a family, and I will bring you to Zion".

37. God Is The Original Avenger
Jeremiah 5:9
"Shall I not punish them for these things?" says the Lord. "And shall I not avenge Myself on such a nation as this"?

38. God Restores Health And Healing
Jeremiah 8:22
Is there no balm in Gilead, Is there no physician there? Why then is there no recovery for the health of the daughter of my people?

Jeremiah 30:17
For I will restore health to you and heal you of your wounds,' says the Lord, 'because they called you an outcast saying: "This is Zion; No one seeks her."'

Isaiah 57:18
I have seen his ways, and will heal him; I will also lead him, and restore comforts to him and to his mourners.

39. God's Desire Is To Restore
Jeremiah 12:15
Then it shall be, after I have plucked them out, that I will return and have compassion on them and bring them back, everyone to his heritage and everyone to his land.

40. God Will Bring Back My Seed From Captivity
Jeremiah 30:10
'Therefore do not fear, O My servant Jacob,' says the Lord, 'Nor be dismayed, O Israel; for behold, I will save you from afar, and your seed from the land of their captivity. Jacob shall return, have rest and be quiet, and no one shall make him afraid.

Amos 9:13-15
"Behold, the days are coming," says the Lord, "When the plowman shall overtake the reaper, and the treader of grapes him who sows seed; the mountains shall drip with sweet wine, and all the hills shall flow with it. 14 I will bring back the captives of My people Israel; they shall

build the waste cities and inhabit them; they shall plant vineyards and drink wine from them; they shall also make gardens and eat fruit from them. 15 I will plant them in their land, and no longer shall they be pulled up from the land I have given them," says the Lord your God.

Deuteronomy 6:11
Houses full of all good things, which you did not fill, hewn-out wells which you did not dig, vineyards and olive trees which you did not plant—when you have eaten and are full.

41. You Renew And Restore Us, Oh Lord
Lamentations 5:21
Turn us back to You, O Lord, and we will be restored; renew our days as of old.

Hosea 6:2
After two days He will revive us; on the third day He will raise us up, that we may live in His sight.

42. God Is Righteous And Brings Justice
Zephaniah 3:5
The Lord is righteous in her midst, He will do no unrighteousness. Every morning He brings His justice to light; He never fails, but the unjust knows no shame.

43. God's Desire Is For Justice And Compassion
Zechariah 7:9-10
Thus says the Lord of hosts: 'Execute true justice, show mercy and compassion everyone to his brother. 10 Do not oppress the widow or the fatherless, the alien or the poor. Let none of you plan evil in his heart against his brother.'

44. God's Promise Is Restoration
Joel 2:25-26
So I will restore to you the years that the swarming locust has eaten, the crawling locust, the consuming locust, and the chewing locust, my great army which I sent among you. 26 You shall eat in plenty and be satisfied, and praise the name of the Lord your God, who has dealt wondrously with you; and My people shall never be put to shame.

45. God Is A God Of Vengeance For His Enemies
Nahum 1:2-3
God is jealous, and the Lord avenges; The Lord avenges and is furious. The Lord will take vengeance on His adversaries, and He reserves wrath for His enemies; 3 The Lord is slow to anger and great in power, and will not at all acquit the wicked. The Lord has His way in the whirlwind and in the storm, and the clouds are the dust of His feet.

46. God's Promise Is To Restore Double
Zechariah 9:12
Return to the stronghold, you prisoners of hope. Even today I declare that I will restore double to you.

47. God's Promise Is To Restore The Hearts Of Families
Malachi 4:6
"And he will turn the hearts of the fathers to the children, and the hearts of the children to their fathers, lest I come and strike the earth with a curse."

48. God Gives Rewards
Matthew 10:41-42
He who receives a prophet in the name of a prophet shall

receive a prophet's reward. And he who receives a righteous man in the name of a righteous man shall receive a righteous man's reward. 42 And whoever gives one of these little ones only a cup of cold water in the name of a disciple, assuredly, I say to you, he shall by no means lose his reward.

49. **God Will Reward According To Man's Works**
Matthew 16:26-27
For what profit is it to a man if he gains the whole world, and loses his own soul? Or what will a man give in exchange for his soul? 27 For the Son of Man will come in the glory of His Father with His angels, and then He will reward each according to his works.

Matthew 7:1-2
Judge not, that you be not judged. 2 For with what judgment you judge, you will be judged; and with the measure you use, it will be measured back to you.

50. **God Rewards Good Stewardship**
Matthew 25:23-30
His lord said to him, 'Well done, good and faithful servant; you have been faithful over a few things, I will make you ruler over many things. Enter into the joy of your lord.' 24 Then he who had received the one talent came and said, 'Lord, I knew you to be a hard man, reaping where you have not sown, and gathering where you have not scattered seed. 25 And I was afraid, and went and hid your talent in the ground. Look, there you have what is yours.' 26 But his lord answered and said to him, 'You wicked and lazy servant, you knew that I reap where I have not sown, and gather where I have not scattered seed. 27 So you ought to have deposited my money with the bankers, and at my coming I would have received

back my own with interest. 28 Therefore take the talent from him, and give it to him who has ten talents. 29 For to everyone who has, more will be given, and he will have abundance; but from him who does not have, even what he has will be taken away. 30 And cast the unprofitable servant into the outer darkness. There will be weeping and gnashing of teeth.'

51. God Sees And Rewards Our Works
Matthew 25:34-46

Then the King will say to those on His right hand, 'Come, you blessed of My Father, inherit the kingdom prepared for you from the foundation of the world: 35 for I was hungry and you gave Me food; I was thirsty and you gave Me drink; I was a stranger and you took Me in; 36 I was naked and you clothed Me; I was sick and you visited Me; I was in prison and you came to Me.' 37 Then the righteous will answer Him, saying, 'Lord, when did we see You hungry and feed You, or thirsty and give You drink? 38 When did we see You a stranger and take You in, or naked and clothe You? 39 Or when did we see You sick, or in prison, and come to You?' 40 And the King will answer and say to them, 'Assuredly, I say to you, inasmuch as you did it to one of the least of these My brethren, you did it to Me.' 41 Then He will also say to those on the left hand, 'Depart from Me, you cursed, into the everlasting fire prepared for the devil and his angels: 42 for I was hungry and you gave Me no food; I was thirsty and you gave Me no drink; 43 I was a stranger and you did not take Me in, naked and you did not clothe Me, sick and in prison and you did not visit Me.' 44 Then they also will answer Him, saying, 'Lord, when did we see You hungry or thirsty or a stranger or naked or sick or in prison, and did not minister to You?' 45 Then He will answer them, saying, 'Assuredly, I say to you, inasmuch as you did not do it to one of the least of these, you did not do it to Me.' 46 And these will go away into everlasting punishment, but the righteous into eternal life."

52. God Will Repay
Mark 10:29-30
So Jesus answered and said, "Assuredly, I say to you, there is no one who has left house or brothers or sisters or father or mother or wife or children or lands, for My sake and the gospel's, 30 who shall not receive a hundredfold now in this time—houses and brothers and sisters and mothers and children and lands, with persecutions—and in the age to come, eternal life".

Luke 18:29-30
So He said to them, "Assuredly, I say to you, there is no one who has left house or parents or brothers or wife or children, for the sake of the kingdom of God, 30 who shall not receive many times more in this present time, and in the age to come eternal life."

53. God Is Restoring The Hearts Of The Children To Their Parents
Luke 1:17
He will also go before Him in the spirit and power of Elijah, 'to turn the hearts of the fathers to the children,' and the disobedient to the wisdom of the just, to make ready a people prepared for the Lord."

Malachi 4:5-6
Behold, I will send you Elijah the prophet before the coming of the great and dreadful day of the LORD. 6 And he will turn the hearts of the fathers to the children, and the hearts of the children to their fathers,

lest I come and strike the earth with a curse.

54. **The Mission Of Jesus Was Restoration - To Restore All That Was Stolen From The Enemy**
Luke 4:18
The Spirit of the Lord is upon Me, because He has anointed Me to preach the gospel to the poor; He has sent Me to heal the brokenhearted, to proclaim liberty to the captives and recovery of sight to the blind, to set at liberty those who are oppressed.

1 John 3:8
He who sins is of the devil, for the devil has sinned from the beginning. For this purpose the Son of God was manifested, that He might destroy the works of the devil.

55. **God Rewards Doing Good**
Luke 6:35
But love your enemies, do good, and lend, hoping for nothing in return; and your reward will be great, and you will be sons of the Most High. For He is kind to the unthankful and evil.

Matthew 5:12
Rejoice and be exceedingly glad, for great is your reward in heaven, for so they persecuted the prophets who were before you.

Colossians 3:23-25
And whatever you do, do it heartily, as to the Lord and not to men, 24 knowing that from the Lord you will receive the reward of the inheritance; for you serve the Lord Christ. 25 But he who does wrong will be repaid for what he has done, and there is no partiality.

56. **It Is God Who Judges**
Luke 16:25
But Abraham said, 'Son, remember that in your lifetime you received your good things, and likewise Lazarus evil things; but now he is comforted and you are tormented'.

Hebrews 12:23
To the general assembly and church of the firstborn who are registered in heaven, to God the Judge of all, to the spirits of just men made perfect.

Romans 3:5-6
But if our unrighteousness demonstrates the righteousness of God, what shall we say? Is God unjust who inflicts wrath? (I speak as a man.) 6 Certainly not! For then how will God judge the world?

57. **The Lord Will Avenge His Own Elect**
Luke 18:4-8
And he would not for a while; but afterward he said within himself, 'Though I do not fear God nor regard man, 5 yet because this widow troubles me I will avenge her, lest by her continual coming she weary me.'" 6 Then the Lord said, "Hear what the unjust judge said. 7 And shall God not avenge His own elect who cry out day and night to Him, though He bears long with them? 8 I tell you that He will avenge them speedily. Nevertheless, when the Son of Man comes, will He really find faith on the earth?"

58. **Vengeance Belongs To The Lord**
Romans 12:19
Beloved, do not avenge yourselves, but rather give place to wrath; for it is written, "Vengeance is Mine, I will repay," says the Lord.

Hebrews 10:30-31
For we know Him who said, "Vengeance is Mine, I will repay," says the Lord. And again, "The Lord will judge His people." 31 It is a fearful thing to fall into the hands of the living God.

59. I Restore Others In Gentleness
Galatians 6:1
Brethren, if a man is overtaken in any trespass, you who are spiritual restore such a one in a spirit of gentleness, considering yourself lest you also be tempted.

1 Corinthians 2:15
But he who is spiritual judges all things, yet he himself is rightly judged by no one.

60. What A Man Sows He Will Reap
Galatians 6:7
Do not be deceived, God is not mocked; for whatever a man sows, that he will also reap.

Job 4:8
Even as I have seen, those who plow iniquity and sow trouble reap the same.

Proverbs 22:8
He who sows iniquity will reap sorrow, and the rod of his anger will fail.

Psalm 126:5-6
Those who sow in tears shall reap in joy. 6 He who continually goes forth weeping, bearing seed for sowing, shall doubtless come again with rejoicing, bringing his sheaves with him.

2 Corinthians 9:10-11
Now may He who supplies seed to the sower, and bread for food, supply and multiply the seed you have sown and increase the fruits of your righteousness, 11 while you are enriched in everything for all liberality, which causes thanksgiving through us to God.

61. **Pay Day Is Coming - God Is The Righteous Judge**
2 Timothy 4:1
I charge you therefore before God and the Lord Jesus Christ, who will judge the living and the dead at His appearing and His kingdom.

2 Timothy 4:8
Finally, there is laid up for me the crown of righteousness, which the Lord, the righteous Judge, will give to me on that Day, and not to me only but also to all who have loved His appearing.

1 Corinthians 4:5
Therefore judge nothing before the time, until the Lord comes, who will both bring to light the hidden things of darkness and reveal the counsels of the hearts. Then each one's praise will come from God.

Revelation 22:11-12
He who is unjust, let him be unjust still; he who is filthy, let him be filthy still; he who is righteous, let him be righteous still; he who is holy, let him be holy still." 12 "And behold, I am coming quickly, and My reward is with Me, to give to every one according to his work".

62. **God Will Judge The Nations**
2 Timothy 4:8
Finally, there is laid up for me the crown of

righteousness, which the Lord, the righteous Judge, will give to me on that Day, and not to me only but also to all who have loved His appearing.

Psalm 96:13
For He is coming, for He is coming to judge the earth. He shall judge the world with righteousness, and the peoples with His truth.

Revelation 11:18
The nations were angry, and Your wrath has come, and the time of the dead, that they should be judged, and that You should reward Your servants the prophets and the saints, and those who fear Your name, small and great, and should destroy those who destroy the earth."

63. **God Is Judge Of All - Not Man**
James 4:11-12
Do not speak evil of one another, brethren. He who speaks evil of a brother and judges his brother, speaks evil of the law and judges the law. But if you judge the law, you are not a doer of the law but a judge. 12 There is one Lawgiver, who is able to save and to destroy. Who are you to judge another?

Hebrews 12:23
To the general assembly and church of the firstborn who are registered in heaven, to God the Judge of all, to the spirits of just men made perfect.

Hebrews 13:4
Marriage is honorable among all, and the bed undefiled; but fornicators and adulterers God will judge.

64. **God Will Bring His Vindication**
Revelation 6:10

And they cried with a loud voice, saying, "How long, O Lord, holy and true, until You judge and avenge our blood on those who dwell on the earth?"

Revelation 18:20
"Rejoice over her, O heaven, and you holy apostles and prophets, for God has avenged you on her!"

Revelation 19:2
For true and righteous are His judgments, because He has judged the great harlot who corrupted the earth with her fornication; and He has avenged on her the blood of His servants shed by her."

65. **God Is The Judge Of All Evil**
Revelation 18:6-8
Render to her just as she rendered to you, and repay her double according to her works; in the cup which she has mixed, mix double for her. 7 In the measure that she glorified herself and lived luxuriously, in the same measure give her torment and sorrow; for she says in her heart, 'I sit as queen, and am no widow, and will not see sorrow.' 8 Therefore her plagues will come in one day-- death and mourning and famine. And she will be utterly burned with fire, for strong is the Lord God who judges her.

Revelation 19:11
Now I saw heaven opened, and behold, a white horse. And He who sat on him was called Faithful and True, and in righteousness He judges and makes war.

1 Peter 4:5
They will give an account to Him who is ready to judge the living and the dead.

CONCLUSION

We don't need to be afraid in these last days. God has made provision for every scenario you may encounter in life. He will take care of you. He is eager to perform His words in your life! I hope this book of Scriptures has given you hope for these troubled times.

If you have never made Jesus Lord of your life, would you like to pray this prayer out loud?

Dear God in Heaven,

I believe that Jesus is Your Son, and that He died on the cross for my sins, and that you raised Him up from the dead. I ask you, Jesus, to come into my heart. I repent for my sin, and I receive you into my heart. I confess you as my Lord and my Savior. God, I believe I am saved. I confess with my mouth that I am saved and born again. I am a child of God! Amen!

ABOUT THE AUTHOR

Jackie May Johnson encourages people to live for Jesus. Rescued out of the New Age world, Jackie has taken the Word of God into her heart in abundance. Her life is filled with testimonies of God's healing power, deliverance and provision. Jackie's passion is to help believers find their destiny and to equip them to do the works of Jesus. A noted author and speaker, Jackie teaches on the integrity of the Word of God. Her field of expertise is prophetic evangelism, and dream interpretation, and she has trained and led many outreach teams. As a former French and English teacher, Jackie has lived, studied and ministered overseas for over 24 years. She and her husband Bob have been married 33 years and have four grown sons and four grandchildren.

Other books by Jackie May Johnson

I Am Loved By God Volume 1
Am I Really Hearing You, God? Volume 3

A Dream Manual for Christians: An Interactive Course In Dream Interpretation

And, her testimony of salvation
My Rescue Story: Out of Darkness into the Light

To contact Jackie May for a speaking engagement or to order any of her other books, please contact her place of ministry:
Encourage And Rescue LLC
(Website under construction)

encourageandrescue@gmail.com

Made in the USA
Columbia, SC
01 November 2017